HABITS *of a* CHILD'S HEART

RAISING YOUR KIDS *with the* SPIRITUAL DISCIPLINES

D0017769

VALERIE E. HESS *and* MARTI WATSON GARLETT, Ph.D.

NAVPRESS®

Bringing Truth to Life

OUR GUARANTEE TO YOU

The Navigators is an international Christian organization. Our mission is to reach, disciple, and equip people to know Christ and to make Him known through successive generations. We envision multitudes of diverse people in the United States and every other nation who have a passionate love for Christ, live a lifestyle of sharing Christ's love, and multiply spiritual laborers among those without Christ.

NavPress is the publishing ministry of The Navigators. NavPress publications help believers learn biblical truth and apply what they learn to their lives and ministries. Our mission is to stimulate spiritual formation among our readers.

© 2004 by Valerie E. Hess and Marti Watson Garlett

All rights reserved. No part of this publication may be reproduced in any form without written permission from NavPress, P.O. Box 35001, Colorado Springs, CO 80935.
www.navpress.com

NAVPRESS, BRINGING TRUTH TO LIFE, and the NAVPRESS logo are registered trademarks of NavPress. Absence of ® in connection with marks of NavPress or other parties does not indicate an absence of registration of those marks.

ISBN 1-57683-427-1

Cover design by The Office of Bill Chiaravalle, www.officeofbc.com, DeAnna Pierce
Cover photo by Brand X Pictures, Photodisc
Creative Team: Terry Behimer, Liz Heaney, Cara Iverson, Pat Miller

Some of the anecdotal illustrations in this book are true to life and are included with the permission of the persons involved. All other illustrations are composites of real situations, and any resemblance to people living or dead is coincidental.

Unless otherwise identified, all Scripture quotations in this publication are taken from the HOLY BIBLE: NEW INTERNATIONAL VERSION® (NIV®). Copyright © 1973, 1978, 1984 by International Bible Society. Used by permission of Zondervan Publishing House. All rights reserved. Other versions used include: the *New Revised Standard Version* (NRSV), copyright © 1989, by the Division of Christian Education of the National Council of the Churches of Christ in the USA, used by permission, all rights reserved; and the *King James Version* (KJV).

Hess, Valerie E., 1954-
  Habits of a child's heart : raising your kids with the spiritual
disciplines / Valerie E. Hess and Marti Watson Garlett.
     p. cm.
Includes bibliographical references.
  ISBN 1-57683-427-1 (pbk.)
  1. Christian education--Home training. 2. Christian
children--Religious life. 3. Spiritual formation. I. Garlett, Marti
Watson, 1945- II. Title.
  BV1590.H465 2004
  248.8'45--dc22

                              2003020500

Printed in the United States of America

1 2 3 4 5 6 7 8 9 10 / 08 07 06 05 04

FOR A FREE CATALOG OF NAVPRESS BOOKS & BIBLE STUDIES,
CALL 1-800-366-7788 (USA) OR 1-416-499-4615 (CANADA)

"*Habits of a Child's Heart* is a book that has been needed for a long, long time. Hess and Garlett break new ground by showing parents how to share their daily walk with Christ with their children."

—DON RATCLIFF, Ph.D., department of education, Biola University; coauthor, *Raising Your Child: From Birth to Age Twelve*

"What a beautiful guide for families to use! Valerie and Marti will help you grow daily in the Word, faith, and acts as your family embarks on a lifelong spiritual journey."

—CAROLYN R. HAUGEN, Ed.D., elder of Christian education, Friday Harbor Presbyterian Church

To John, for modeling this book to me for twenty-eight years.
— VALERIE

To my first-ever daughter, Yan, and to the prospect of my second daughter, Carrie: I love both of you dearly and bless the day you each came into our family. You have enlarged it in very special ways and made all of us more complete.
— MARTI

CONTENTS

ACKNOWLEDGMENTS

VALERIE:

Our lives are never lived in isolation. One person's action can change the whole course of our lives. For that reason, I'd like to thank Jean Fuller, who gave my husband, John, *Celebration of Discipline* years ago. I can still picture the vacation condo living room where John said to me, "You might be interested in reading this." His hunches have blessed me for many years now.

I also want to thank the numerous Sunday school class members, workshop participants, and local Renovaré groups who have shared with me their stories of learning to be better disciples of Jesus Christ. They have sharpened my thinking on the disciplines with hard questions and public accountability. It is because of their desire to know how to share these truths with their children that this book was conceived.

I thank Reverend Gwen Brown and Kathy Raybin for being my longtime Renovaré partners; Barb Steiner, who has processed so much with me; Judy Schulz, who has taught me so much about Christian living in all circumstances; and my children, Maggie Rogers and Lydia Hess, who continue to teach me about unconditional love. There have been numerous church members and staff who have modeled discipleship to me throughout my life. God knows what role each of them has played in my faith formation and will reward them well for it.

I am grateful to Terry Behimer of NavPress for her continued faith in this project and to our wonderful editor, Liz Heaney, who helped us pull all the loose ends together. And finally, I thank Richard and Carolynn Foster for their work and witness. Their shared wisdom and friendship mean more than words can say.

❧ ❧ ❧

MARTI:

No book is written without support. My support team begins with my husband, Fred, to whom I've been married for thirty-eight years and counting. You allow me to be who I am, never trying to change me, and instead you unfailingly, unselfishly encourage me in all my personal and professional challenges and gladly take on many burdens so that I may have protected time to work and reflect. I will love you eternally.

Almost everything I've learned about parenting—and life— that is truly profound is because I was taught it firsthand throughout the thirty-six-plus years of raising Marc and Kyle, the lights of my life, the two souls etched everlastingly onto my heart. Words cannot express what each of you means to me and how much I owe you for all that you have brought into my life. Because of you, I am the person I am today. I love you fiercely, as perhaps only a mother can.

I am grateful to Lynda Graybeal for bringing Valerie and me together to write this book. It would have been almost impossible to span the miles between Colorado and California without you, Lynda. Thank you for your help. Also, thank you, Tom Zane, for your generosity and computer graphics expertise.

And to our editor, Liz Heaney—this is the second book I've been blessed to work on with you—a resounding thank-you for wisdom, patience, and enduring friendship. The ideas may be ours, but the fact that the book has become what it is owes much to you, Liz. Frankly, I can't even imagine working on another book without your guiding hand resting on my shoulder and providing me with focused inspiration.

I would be remiss if I didn't especially thank Richard Foster for his faith in me throughout the many years I've known him. We met in the early fall of 1978 when we were both new faculty colleagues; I literally learned the spiritual disciplines directly from you over many years of sharing weekly lunches in our beloved Milton Center group. Because of you, I celebrate always, even in times of great sorrow and fear, of which (as you know) our family has had much. God brought you into my life, and I have never been the same since. Thank you for equal doses of laughter and prayer, Richard. My mind is filled now and ever with memories of your friendship and ministry to me.

INTRODUCTION

This is what the LORD says:
"Stand at the crossroads and look;
ask for the ancient paths,
ask where the good way is, and walk in it,
and you will find rest for your souls."

JEREMIAH 6:16

All of us—young or old, new Christians or mature in the faith—
can benefit from the strengths and freedoms the spiritual disciplines bring. We know, because the two of us have experienced
firsthand their value in nurturing spiritual maturity and deepening
connection with God.

Our prayer is that this book you hold in your hands will inspire
you to begin practicing the disciplines in your own life, if you
aren't already doing so, and then show you how to cultivate the
life-affirming possibilities of the spiritual disciplines—or "holy
habits," as they're sometimes known—in your children.

Please don't be put off by the word *discipline*. While the word certainly involves correction, it does not involve punishment. It comes
directly from the Latin *disciplina*, which connotes "giving instruction
to a disciple." When we personally practice the disciplines, we are
inviting God to change us, to make us more like his Son, and to

"correct" how we live our lives in community with others, God, and the world. When we teach children the spiritual disciplines, we are giving spiritual instruction to young disciples, people who will grow up to imitate much more of what we *do* than what we *say*.

Start praying now about introducing the disciplines into your family's life. Keep a journal of family activities for a week. What issues do your children struggle with? What issues do *you* struggle with? What are the issues behind those issues? If your kids are cranky at night, are they picking up your stress? Where do things run smoothly? What would you change about yourself and your family rhythms if you could? Why? By posing prayerfully asked questions and keeping track of observations, each of us can find a beginning point.

Nondiscipleship costs abiding peace, a life penetrated throughout by love, faith that sees everything in the light of God's governance for good, hope that stands firm in the most discouraging of circumstances, power to do what is right and withstand the forces of evil. In short it costs exactly that abundance of life Jesus said he came to bring (John 10:10).

DALLAS WILLARD

How to Use This Book

While this book is a joint venture, Marti wrote the odd-numbered chapters, and Valerie wrote the even-numbered chapters and the appendix.

As you begin, rest assured that there's no right or wrong way to work through these materials. Remain open to the Holy Spirit. Start with a discipline that you are somewhat familiar with; you don't need to work through this book sequentially, although it certainly can be read that way. There's nothing sacred about a discipline's positioning. Each one relates closely to the others; they're supportive and complementary. Keep in mind that each discipline eventually must be acted upon individually to achieve spiritual balance, which means we can't skip those that seem difficult or uncomfortable.

Be sensitive to the Holy Spirit's leading so that you don't allow the spiritual disciplines to become "one more activity" in your family life—along with soccer, ballet, and piano lessons. If they lead to legalism or a "holier-than-thou" pride, discontinue their use immediately. We don't gain heavenly points for knowing how to "do" the disciplines correctly. As a parent, your job is to bring sanity to all aspects of family life so that walking the talk—or as Scripture puts it, seeking first the kingdom of God—can actually happen.

That's why we've started each chapter with two sections specifically for adults: "Understanding the Discipline" and "Practicing the Discipline." These sections are intended to help ground you in the discipline and begin practicing it before you move to the final section of the chapter, "Teaching the Discipline." There we've outlined age-specific ideas and exercises you can do with your children to help them grasp the concepts. The section is organized into Early Childhood (ages 4–7), Middle Childhood (ages 8–11), and Adolescence (ages 12–15). However, because there's a variation in abilities and maturity levels in kids, use parental discretion. Scan all activities suggested and use only what you think would work in your situation. Also, our suggestions are not exhaustive. There's plenty of room for creativity. Allow your children as much input as possible.

The most effective way we can teach our kids is in the context of our daily lives, and this is certainly true of the disciplines. As Deuteronomy 6:6-9 tells us, "These commandments that I give you today are to be upon your hearts. Impress them on your children. Talk about them when you sit at home and when you walk along the road, when you lie down and when you get up. Tie them as symbols on your hands and bind them on your foreheads. Write them on the doorframes of your houses and on your gates." The spiritual disciplines are meant to become a significant part of our lives and not some exotic add-on. We wrote this book to help you find ways to incorporate them into your lives and conversations.

The goal of the disciplines is to place us in a position where the Holy Spirit can do God's transforming work in us. Pursue them as a means to bring about significant change in your inner and outer lives and to model them for your children. Build them into your life and into your children's lives until you have covered all twelve disciplines—and then start over. We never master the spiritual disciplines; they are holy habits to last a lifetime.

Welcome to life on the frontiers of the faith!

My Lord God, I have no idea where I am going. I do not see the road ahead of me.

I cannot know for certain where it will end. Nor do I really know myself, and the fact that I think that I am following your will does not mean that I am actually doing so. But I believe that the desire to please you does in fact please you. And I hope I have that desire in all that I am doing.

I hope that I will never do anything apart from that desire.

And I know that if I do this you will lead me by the right road though I may know nothing about it. Therefore will I trust you always though I may seem to be lost and in the shadow of death. I will not fear, for you are ever with me, and you will never leave me to face my perils alone.

THOMAS MERTON

Chapter One

THE DISCIPLINE OF MEDITATION

I meditate on your precepts
and consider your ways.
I delight in your decrees;
I will not neglect your word.

PSALM 119:15-16

UNDERSTANDING THE DISCIPLINE

The Discipline of Meditation helps us focus on hearing God's voice. Meditation teaches us to become like tea bags, soaking deeply and quietly in God and his Word so that we can better hear him speak to our hearts and minds. And, as a gentleman named Earl learned, sometimes we stumble upon this knowledge serendipitously.

In California's San Gabriel Mountains, there is a path known to locals as the Garcia Trail. It rises 866 vertical feet per mile above the valley floor and offers stunning views at its summit. When Earl reached his fiftieth birthday, he decided he would hike the Garcia Trail fifty times during the year in an effort to stretch the physical limits of his aging body and regain, at least in part, the stamina of his youth. He reached his goal with an additional serendipity—a quiet, meditative time each week alone with God.

On Saturday at dawn, he left his house while his family still slept, packed a breakfast burrito and a palm-sized Bible, and ascended into the Angeles National Forest. Flat rocks at the crest gave Earl both a bench and a table for eating his simple breakfast and contemplating a small but significant portion of the creation given to him by the Lord of the universe. He also read Scripture and prayed.

The quiet permeating Earl's mountaintop morning brought him closer to God, from the stilling of the beat of his exercised heart to deliberate focus on the taste of each morsel of his breakfast to intentional honoring of each muscle's slow cooldown as amazing organic gifts from his Maker. Earl often wondered at his corporeal body, how it worked and flexed, how the senses God built into it combined to allow him existence as a human being but also enriched his physical life with sensation. In contemplating his own physiology, Earl learned more about the One who had fashioned it, and his own bodily workings struck him with as much awe and majesty as the mountain did.

Most mornings, Earl settled in like this for an hour or more, reluctant to leave what had now become a much-anticipated time alone in God's company. As a result of this time spent in meditation, Earl attained a new and surprising intimacy with his Creator.

Meditation sends us into our ordinary world
with greater perspective and balance.

RICHARD FOSTER

Transcending Life Circumstances

Through meditation, we center ourselves on God. This discipline enables us to locate, and more rapidly return to, an internal core within ourselves where we know God will be waiting. As we center our thoughts on God, we allow him to comfort us and invite us to trust him in the dark.

He did this for me (Marti) on a starless night shortly after our then-teenaged son Kyle was diagnosed with the form of lymphatic cancer called Hodgkin's disease. I found myself wandering sleeplessly through our still house, trapped in a wretched state of mind. I had no idea how I could get through this fearsome diagnosis for Kyle and all its horrific implications. The future I was so certain was laid out for my talented son suddenly contained an abyss with an unfathomable and frightening potential ending. No human being could help me or bring me the comfort I craved—not my husband, not my pastor, not my dearest friends. No, my soul had to face its long night of suffering alone—except, of course, for the presence of God.

But as I faced down those cold hours of darkness, tears spilling down my face, no prayers would come—only deep internal groanings. So I did the one thing I knew to do: I picked up my Bible, felt its heft in my hand, took in the reassuring scent of its leather binding, and began reading through Psalms. I found verses penned by similarly tortured hearts, and, in their open acknowledgment of foreboding and despair and their pleas for mercy and victory, an odd sort of comfort seeped into my soul.

As if I had no time to waste, I hurriedly began writing down verses on three-by-five-inch index cards that spoke to, simultaneously, fear of enemies and trust in God. I then went all over the house taping the cards on mirrors, walls, door posts, and even (in the bathroom Kyle used) under the toilet seat lid. As I meditated on those words, God soothed my anxious heart. Finally, I found myself able to crawl back in bed beside my husband and sleep.

Spending Satisfied Time Alone with God

Meditation insists on taking focused time—lots of it—to listen to what God has to say to us personally. There is no express-lane version of this discipline, no microwave edition of finding and spending quiet time with him. Instead, meditation slow-cooks like a Crock-Pot, requiring deep reflection on a biblical word, phrase, or concept.

Several years ago I spent three months in Korea, teaching English to college-aged young women and Korean military officers. God was my only companion on this trip, and I spent countless hours with him. I spoke aloud to him in my apartment and intensely felt his ever-present nearness. He was my guard against loneliness, which at every turn threatened to overpower me. Those were, without a doubt, some of the most satisfying months I ever spent with my Creator. Upon my return to American life, I realized how easy it is for me to let Western clamor invade my 24/7 cherished relationship with God. I have had to work fiercely to guard against the seduction of stateside culture and protect my hard-won intimacy with God.

In the Discipline of Meditation, we slow down and focus on God—and we gain increasing ability to hear God's holy voice through his manifold methods of communication.

God Speaks in Various Ways

Meditation requires us to remain creatively open to how God may speak to us. True learning requires uninhibited awe and wonder, much like that of a child. Each of us is ever a small child as we continually, throughout all the days of our lives, attempt to learn more and more about God.

Among the communication tools in God's hamper are nature, art, music, books, and even, on occasion, current events. When we intentionally and deliberately learn from these things, God can use them to speak to us personally. Often this leads toward self-selected fields of formal study, which we will cover in more detail in chapter 4, "The Discipline of Study."

Valerie lives in the foothills of the Rocky Mountains above Boulder, Colorado, and has daily opportunities for nature walks that help her turn her focus away from busyness, toward God and God alone. During her walks, she asks God to speak to her through the created splendor of her surroundings. One time in particular stands out in her mind.

After a slight from a friend, Valerie paid no attention to her environs, walking wearily with her head down. Unheralded, she walked into a field of wildflowers that had not been blooming the last time she had taken this particular trail. Now they were a stunningly gorgeous bouquet practically placed in her lap, flowers that would hardly be seen by human eyes in this remote area, flowers that were doing what they were created to do—radiantly blossom for the glory of God and no one else. She realized that was the message God intended for her to receive—that like those flowers, she was created to do and be wholly herself, no matter whether others noticed or nodded approvingly.

————————

Unless we change our direction, we are likely to
end up where we are headed.

CHINESE PROVERB

————————

Growth of a Peaceful Center

When we hear God speaking to us, we are better able to discern his will, which helps us become less frantic and more likely to access the solid, calm center that Jesus manifested. In the Discipline of Meditation, we seek to hear God's voice directly. If all we ever do is listen to someone else interpret God's Word for us—and there certainly are many times when that is appropriate—then we will never encounter the living God ourselves.

Nothing in our lives will keep us healthier than learning how to develop and hold on to a peaceful center. If we can do this—and we can—we are no longer helpless victims to life's ups and downs. To be sure, some things we don't want to happen will, and some things we wish would happen won't. But the calm center provided through meditation instills in us an ability to respond appropriately to whatever comes our way and greet it with God's eyes and perspective.

If you long to have a deeper relationship with God, then find a quiet spot and a small portion of Scripture and spend time with those words every day for several days. Have a cup of tea to help you remember to steep in this deliberately carved-out, contemplative moment.

Where there is peace and meditation,
there is neither anxiety nor doubt.

ST. FRANCIS OF ASSISI

PRACTICING THE DISCIPLINE

When we quiet our hearts and slow down to meditate, we are more apt to hear God's voice. God can work on, with, and for you during any of the activities that follow. Before you bring your children into the mix, we strongly urge you to strengthen your own inward ability to meditate.

1. Take a verse of Scripture or even just a phrase from a verse. When you read the verse, do so with intentionality and deliberateness. Don't rush. Reflect on the verse a while. Ask yourself questions such as: *How does this verse read when I insert my own name into it as if God were speaking directly to me and no one else? What is the context for this verse? How does it fit with those that surround it?* Write the verse on index cards and tape them in your kitchen, car, and office. Spend a week listening for what God may be saying through those words about him, you, or your life circumstances. Replace this concentrated meditation the next week by selecting a different verse.

2. Meditate on the local and international events of our world and listen to what God may be saying in and through them. Is the media representing a biblical viewpoint? Is American culture

synonymous with God's preferred lifestyle? Why are there so
many different cultures represented on earth throughout the mil-
lennia since God's creation? What does that say about God's love
of diversity? Are American interests abroad synchronized with
God's leading? Ask the Holy Spirit to give you God's heart and
perspective on local, national, and global issues. Think about
what you would do in a certain situation if you were in charge.

3. Practice the ancient Israelite art of *lectio divina.* In *lectio divina*
we listen for the still, small voice of God, that "gentle whisper"
(1 Kings 19:12) that is God's Word for us, God's voice touching
our hearts. This tender listening is an atunement to the presence of God in Scripture. We try to imitate the prophet Elijah,
knowing that we must "hear" the voice of God, which often
speaks very softly. In order to hear someone speaking softly, we
must learn to love silence. If we are constantly speaking or if
we are surrounded with noise, we cannot hear gentle sounds.
The practice of *lectio divina*, therefore, requires that we first
quiet down in order to hear God's Word to us. This is the first
step of *lectio divina*, appropriately called *lectio,* or "reading."

   In *lectio* we read slowly and attentively, gently listening to
hear a word or phrase that is God's Word for us this day.
Once we have found a word or passage in the Scriptures that
speaks to us in a personal way, we must take it in and rumi-
nate on it. The image of an animal quietly chewing its cud
was used in antiquity as a symbol of the believer pondering
the Word of God.

4. Carve out quiet time for yourself every single day, even if it is

only ten minutes. Sit somewhere apart from others that can become, for those ten minutes, your space. Deliberately and intentionally work to still the beating of your heart, the rapid thoughts and to-do lists running through your mind. If possible, plug in a small environmental fountain nearby and allow your ears to cease listening to external noise. Breathe deeply; close your eyes; will your body to relax. Then put into your mind a mental image of Christ soothing your brow, of his strong carpenter hands kneading the back of your neck and the tops of your shoulders. Over one or two weeks' time, notice how much you look forward to these few minutes of respite from a wearying day and how refreshed you feel afterward. Know that God has been with you.

TEACHING THE DISCIPLINE

Once you are comfortable with your own meditative abilities, begin teaching the Discipline of Meditation to your children. What follow are several ideas, a menu of choices that are developmentally organized according to children's ages and maturity levels.

EARLY CHILDHOOD (ages 4–7):

1. Take a nature walk with your children. Go to a nearby park and study the plants and flowers. See how many small creatures you can find. Keep a numerical tally. Ask your children to proceed on this walk very quietly, with their ears and eyes open but not their mouths. Then go to a bench or picnic table—or a cloth on the ground—and talk about what you've

seen, including that God is the Creator of it all. Ask your kids to thank God for his creation by writing him a thank-you letter. Write down your children's words exactly as they say them to you. This will help them not only own the experience but also enrich their reading vocabulary. Save this thank-you card in a special place, such as a bookshelf, so that you and your children can reread it on occasion.

2. Buy some bubble bath, tape a picture of Jesus and a phrase like "Jesus loves you" on the wall above the tub, and have your child soak in both. Help your child imagine he or she is soaking in God.

3. Play music your children know and love, but this time, instead of singing with the music, ask them to stay perfectly still and listen to the words. Ask them not to move or talk but to just listen quietly. Follow up by asking them to describe what they were thinking about while the music played.

4. Seat your kids in a safe place, such as a high stool away from the stovetop, and let them watch you cook pasta. Show them how hard the noodles are before going into the water. Pull out a couple after three minutes and, with a fork, let your children see how the noodles are beginning to soften. As you eat the pasta, talk about how meditating on the things of God softens our hearts like the pasta being softened in the boiling water.

MIDDLE CHILDHOOD *(ages 8–11):*

You can expand on any of the ideas found in the Early Childhood section. In addition:

1. Get eight heat-proof cups and two black tea bags. Fill all the cups with boiling water. (Obviously, the younger the child, the greater the need to supervise this exercise.) Put one tea bag in one of the cups. Use the other tea bag to make tea out of the remaining seven cups of water. Set a timer for one minute. During that time, one tea bag will be steeping quietly in the water. The other tea bag will have to be dunked in seven cups in order to make tea in them all. When the timer goes off, take the tea bags out and compare the darkness of the tea in each cup. One should be much darker than the other seven. Talk about why that may be. Then discuss how we can be like the first tea bag when we are reading from God's Word.

    Another way to look at this exercise is to think of us as being the hot water and the Word of God the tea bag. Again, the longer the tea bag soaks in us, the more we become stained with the likeness of God. Paste a picture of a tea bag on the inside of your child's Bible, or provide an actual tea bag to use as a bookmark. Scatter some loose tea leaves among the pages. Review with your children the symbolism of the tea and how it can remind them to read their Bible slowly.

2. Kids in this age group are not too young to learn the ancient tradition called *lectio divina*. Train your children to use their imagination while they listen to you read passages from Scripture. Because *lectio divina* is a slow and measured reading, choose an active story from the Bible, such as Daniel and the lions' den. Read the story aloud in a hushed and reverential

way. Ask your children what stands out, providing adequate
think-time. Children must be helped to approach the Bible this
way; it doesn't come naturally to any of us. And remember,
there are no right or wrong answers.

   After all have had a chance to respond, read the story aloud
again. This time ask what the setting looked like, what the
lions sounded like, what the expression on Daniel's face was
when he was thrown in the den, what the king and his court
looked like, and so on. Do not allow anyone to belittle
another's comments. Finally, read the story aloud one additional time, and then give everyone a chance to share what he
or she heard as a personal message from the story. One person
may hear the need for courage, while another may hear the
need to trust God in the face of death.

3. Scripture memorization is important in the Discipline of
   Meditation. Try to select age-appropriate verses, especially
   verses that can be recalled when negative peer pressure or fear
   of the dark intrudes. Proverbs and Isaiah are filled with them.
   One example is Isaiah 2:5: "Come, O house of [insert your last
   name here], let us walk in the light of the LORD." Other
   examples are the first line of Isaiah 41:10, "Do not fear, for I
   [God] am with you," or this line from Proverbs 17:17: "A
   friend loves at all times." After your children memorize the
   verse, encourage them to spend several days thinking about
   how it applies to their lives today. Discuss how God uses the
   Bible to shape our thoughts, words, and deeds.

ADOLESCENCE *(ages 12–15)*:

Children entering puberty are likely to be uninterested in participating in any of the "Middle Childhood" activities with their younger siblings unless you ask them to lead the activity. Young teens and those edging toward and through adolescence need protected time with you that they don't have to share with younger siblings.

1. Take each of your adolescent youngsters on an overnight camping trip, if at all possible. The best way to do this is with one adult taking one child, but, of course, this isn't always possible; sometimes even an overnight isn't possible. Make it an early morning or late evening trip to the park, if that works better, or camp in your very own backyard. Listen to sounds together, sitting quietly and conversing in low voices, and contemplate the dawn's colors or the evening stars.

    An afternoon fishing excursion can substitute, as can an afternoon picnic or cookout. Find a quiet place, one where your kids do not normally hang out with their friends. (They are likely to be reluctant to have their friends see them with you.) The point of this outing is to observe the smallest details of the world around you and quietly contemplate each element, calling each other's attention to minute observations— the stamen or pistil of a flower, the veins in one leaf that are similar to, yet always different from, the veins in another. What does such mystery and beauty, not to mention originality, say about the mind of its Creator?

2. Parents are their children's first connection to God. Through us

they learn to bond to him. Our teachings help instill his. And our kids will listen to us best if we form bonds with them that are individualized to each youngster, away from a collective group, especially when they have reached adolescence. Thus, we must all try to schedule regular alone times with each of our young teens.

When I was in graduate school and often taking evening classes, I had a standing lunch date with each of my two sons during the week. I made arrangements ahead of time with the school office to pick up one of my sons from school during lunch, and then I would take my other son on a different day. I often packed a sack lunch so that we could find a nearby park and eat together, and other times we would just sit on the hood of our car in a parking lot.

These were not long breaks, but they helped build strong connections from which thoughtful interactions could occur and continue to occur now that both of my sons are grown. Sometimes I introduced a concept or troubling issue from local, national, or world news for us to discuss and contemplate. Sometimes we talked about disturbing issues at school and pondered why a person might behave the way she or he had.

We chewed on these kinds of questions: What values had been exhibited? Were those values found in the Garlett home? Why, or why not? In what ways do our moral standards represent God's? How do we know? What can we do to be sure we are exemplifying for others God's principles for living? Such questions can help set up future research that we will do together, such as finding words in a Bible concordance and then reading the verses we are referred to.

3. Ask your adolescents to join you in a reading club. Commit to a schedule and read a book rich in Christian symbolism, such as C. S. Lewis's *The Lion, the Witch, and the Wardrobe*, part of a seven-book series collectively known as THE CHRONICLES OF NARNIA. Aslan, the Lion, is the Christ character, the Lion of Judah found in Revelation 5:5: "Behold, the *Lion* of the Tribe of Judah, the Root of David, hath prevailed" (KJV, emphasis added). After reading the first book, you might want to continue your reading club commitment to include the next book in the series, then the next, and eventually all of them.

Together you can explore Internet links such as www.narnia.com or http://cslewis.drzeus.net, a site designated "Into the Wardrobe," hosted by Lewis's stepson. Sometimes websites change their Internet addresses without warning. If the ones listed here are not accessible, do a Web search for the word *Narnia*, and lots of new and different sites will be found for you.

4. Encourage your teens to read through a chapter of the Bible at a slow, soaking pace. Remember, we are dealing with the story of God's working among people and not conducting a speed-reading course. Be sensitive to your teens' needs in this regard. Children of all ages have lots of questions about the Bible, especially if they are reading from the Bible itself and not from a Bible storybook.

God's Word contains some weird, brutal, and troubling incidents that baffle adults who have pondered them for years.

Instead of insisting the chapter be finished because of some arbitrary timetable, let the questions come. So what if only one verse or phrase is read and discussed? Our kids will remember it far longer and at a deeper level than if we insist on finishing a chapter for the sake of finishing a chapter. Too often we encourage productivity rather than fruitfulness in our kids. We push them to read the whole Bible within a certain period of time so they can win the award at Sunday school when we should be using the Bible to mold future thoughts and actions.

While it's good to read large sections of Scripture in one sitting for overall content, too many of us stop there. We read so that we can check it off our to-do list for the day. Instead, we might do better to soak in the vast expanses of God's Word from which we will always gather a rich harvest of the fruit of the Spirit: love, joy, peace, patience, kindness, goodness, faithfulness, gentleness, and self-control (see Galatians 5:22-23). Allow your older children to seek deeper meaning in the conflicted feelings many Bible passages arouse in all of us. Encourage them to read Scripture while prayerfully asking God what he wants to say to them through his Word.

THE BOTTOM LINE

The Discipline of Meditation can help you and your children find your way to a new and surprising intimacy with God. That is its essential purpose and the result promised to you for your faithful practice of the discipline.

Chapter Two

THE DISCIPLINE OF PRAYER

One day Peter and John were going up to the temple at the
time of prayer — at three in the afternoon.

ACTS 3:1

UNDERSTANDING THE DISCIPLINE

I (Valerie) was wrestling with elements of my faith. It felt like the
end of a nine-month pregnancy, those days when it is time to give
birth to something new and yet a time of being scared of the
birthing process. I felt restless and antsy in my faith community,
sensing that I should somehow be "getting more out of worship."
I wanted a fuller experience of God, though I didn't exactly know
how to define what that meant. I wondered how I could feel
closer to God and be more open to what he might be calling me
to do. Then I wondered if those were even the right things to
wonder about.

At the suggestion of a friend, I went to visit an Eastern
Orthodox Christian nun gifted in spiritual direction. After only a
few minutes of listening to me try to articulate what I wanted guidance for, she interrupted me with these words: "What is your
rule?" I looked at her blankly. I had no idea what she was talking
about. She repeated, "What is your rule?" When I confessed to not

having one because I didn't know what it was, she patiently explained that I needed to develop a rule of prayer, which is simply a set time and order for prayer each day. She went on to say that a disciplined approach to communicating regularly and intentionally with God would deepen my connection to him and result in better communication with him. She was right.

I need a firm discipline of prayer. We like to pray accord-
ing to our moods — briefly, at length, or not at all. But
that is to be arbitrary. Prayer is not a free-will offering
to God; it is an obligatory service, something God
requires. We are not free to engage in it according to our
own wishes. Prayer is the first divine service in the day.
God requires that we take time for this service.

DIETRICH BONHOEFFER

A Rule of Prayer

Day and night, men and women in monastic communities all over the world gather together for regular times of prayer. At the ringing of a bell or the banging of a hammer on resonant wood, the community stops its work or arises out of sleep and meets together to pray. Sometimes these prayer services last for nearly an hour, such as Lauds in the early morning, and other times they only take a few minutes, such as Compline at bedtime or Vigils at midnight.

While it may be impossible for most of us to follow a monastic time schedule, we can still develop our own rule of prayer by setting aside a regular time each day to pray and by finding a prayer structure that works for us. This enables us to know when we will pray each day and what prayers we will use to help us. When we practice a rule of prayer, prayer gradually becomes a holy habit, something we do that is not dependent on feelings or moods or our ability to articulate well. It becomes central to our lives and strengthens our connections to God.

After my conversation with the Orthodox nun, I began a rule of prayer that has evolved over the years. My rule uses a mixture of prayers written by other people and my own words based on the needs of those around me. One written prayer from my rule that has come to be very important to me is this:

——————————————

O Lord, grant me to greet the coming day in peace.
Help me in all things to rely on your holy will.
In every hour of the day reveal your will to me.
Bless my dealings with all who surround me.
Teach me to treat all that comes to me throughout
the day with peace of soul
and with the firm conviction that your will governs all.
In all my deeds and words guide my thoughts and feelings.
In unforeseen events let me not forget that all are sent by you.
Teach me to act firmly and wisely,
without embittering and embarrassing others.
Give me strength to bear the fatigue of this coming day
with all that it shall bring.
Direct my will, teach me to pray, pray you yourself in me.
Amen.[1]

Even as I continue to pray for needs that arise throughout the day, my rule of prayer in the morning sets the tone for those prayers. And in those days when I don't pray much after my morning rule has ended, I am comforted knowing that at least I had some connection with God in the day.

The way we practice our rule of prayer should be appropriate to the season of life we are in. Mine now takes about thirty minutes, but I no longer have small children at home. I do my rule in the morning, but others do it at midday or at night. A rule can be as simple as saying the Lord's Prayer before getting up and again before going to bed, and can always be added to or subtracted from. The important thing is to develop a regular time of prayer and have at least one prewritten prayer to start that prayer time, one that we will stick to and that will "prime our prayer pump."

Priming the Prayer Pump

Over the seventeen hundred years of Christian monasticism, members of the community must have, at times, become frustrated that they had to stop what they were doing to pray. I'm sure they had times when they didn't feel like praying, for all the same reasons we sometimes struggle with prayer, but the rule of prayer for their community took precedence over their feelings. The same can be true for us.

Particularly during those times when we don't feel like praying or don't know how to pray, an initial written prayer from another source can help us turn racing thoughts away from what we were just doing and shift our focus to God. By sticking to our schedule and structure, we remind our spirits of God's grace and love, even when that grace and love seem far away.

When prayer fades out, power fades out. We are as spiritual as we are prayerful; no more, no less.

E. STANLEY JONES

Several years ago, Marti's son Kyle was diagnosed with chemotherapy-induced leukemia (his second form of cancer). Friends held a healing prayer service for him, but at the time, Marti was away on business. At the time of the prayer service, she went into a small Episcopal church. Here's her description of what happened next:

> As sobs engulfed me, I did not know how to pray. In the pews of the church were hymnals and the *Book of Common Prayer*. In my anguish and fear, I began to read the words of the hymns and use prayers found in the section "Ministration to the Sick" in the *Book of Common Prayer*. The one I prayed most fervently was:
>
> "O God, the strength of the weak and the comfort of sufferers: Mercifully accept our prayers and grant to your servant [Kyle] the help of your power that his sickness may be turned into health and our sorrow into joy, through Jesus Christ our Lord. Amen." [2]
>
> Those words became my words as I joined the prayer

service for Kyle miles away. I left that church feeling at peace, knowing that God loved Kyle even more than I did.

Even when our needs are not as dramatic as Marti's were that day, we can flesh out our "vocabulary of prayer" by using prayers that have been written down from Christians of every time and culture. Just as we help our children expand their vocabularies by reading to them and engaging them in conversations, we expand our vocabularies of prayer by making other people's prayers our own. Hymnals, denominational prayer books, and books of prayers from Christian people in all cultures and time periods can enrich our own prayer lives as we hear new ways of expressing old needs or experience a fresh perspective of how to pray for a situation.

Our rule of prayer can also prime our pump so that we pray "javelin prayers" throughout the day. This ancient phrase refers to the quick prayers we say on the run:

- Jesus, help me remember the answer to this test question.
- God, help me to love this grumpy clerk.
- Lord, show me how to help this frustrated customer.

Javelin prayers are strongest when our structured time of prayer gives focus to them.

To see someone is to pray for them.

FRANK LAUBACH

One line from the prayer I quoted a few pages back that often influences my javelin prayers is, "Teach me to act firmly and wisely, without embittering and embarrassing others." As I pray throughout the day, this line reminds me that I may need to pray for someone I may have "embittered or embarrassed." Or, as I go into a tough situation, I turn the phrase "embittered or embarrassed" into a prayer: "Lord, help me to have this hard conversation in a way that brings glory to you. May I not embitter or embarrass this person even as I have to point out errors in his [or her] work."

By making time in our schedule to pray regularly and by supplementing our own prayers—long and short—with the prayers of other Christians, we deepen our connection to God such that prayer becomes deeply ingrained in our thoughts and heart.

Practicing the Discipline

Begin by assessing your prayer life. If you never have used other people's prayers on a regular basis, consider balancing your prayers with prayers used by Christians in other times and places. If you are afraid to pray without using a prayer written by someone else, experiment with simple phrases that lift up a person or a need. By developing a variety of ways to pray and by having good prayer resources to use, you can strengthen your own prayer life and, ultimately, that of your children.

1. Over a period of time, develop a rule of prayer that works for you. What is the best time of day to have a set time for prayer? Where? At home? In the car? At your desk at work? Will you

stand, sit, or kneel? How will you structure your prayer time
after the opening prewritten prayer? How long will it last?
What will you do when you travel?

2. Find a book of prayers, such as the *Book of Common Prayer*,
   which Marti referred to, or a hymnal or prayer book from a
   liturgical church. Ask your local Christian bookstore for suggestions or check in your local library. Denominational book-
   stores are also good places to find this kind of material and
   often can be accessed online. Commit to using one of the
   prayers every day for a period of time. For instance, find a
   prayer for use during Advent, which starts four Sundays before
   Christmas Day, switch to another prayer for the Twelve Days of
   Christmas, and then do a third one for Epiphany, which starts
   on January 6 and goes through Ash Wednesday (a variable date
   listed on most calendars). That prayer also could help you
   focus on the way the church marks time, a way rarely followed
   by our culture.

3. Establish a very simple rule of prayer by saying the Lord's
   Prayer at nine o'clock in the morning, at noon, and at three in
   the afternoon. The early church used these times to remember
   when Christ was nailed to the cross and the Holy Spirit
   descended (9 A.M.), when the sky was darkened on Good
   Friday and when Peter saw the vision recorded in Acts 10
   (noon), and when Christ died (3 P.M.). Figure out a way to
   remind yourself that it is time to stop and pray. For example, if
   you are at home, use a stove timer that allows you to set it for
   a three-hour time period, or set the alarm on your watch.

Maybe you need to tweak the rule so that you pray as soon as the kids get off to school, at lunchtime, and right before the kids come home from school. Or say it during your morning commute to work, during your lunch break, and during your commute home at the end of the workday.

4. Begin to keep a regular prayer journal. Marti and her husband have done this for years. On one side of the journal, write down specific prayer requests for needs you perceive in your children and other loved ones as well as around the neighborhood, nation, and world. As you discern answers, use the opposite side of the journal to record them across from the original request. Expect that some prayer requests will have an empty space next to them for a very long time, but most eventually fill in with some sort of response, if only a notation that leads you to a new way of forming the request. A prayer journal allows you to track in a very real and wonderful sense how God is working side by side with you in your daily prayer life.

5. Create your own prayer book. Write down prayers you like or that you find yourself praying after reading a passage of Scripture. I have done this for years and now have several of my own handwritten prayer books.

6. Commit to saying javelin prayers as you move through your day. Ask God to help you see the real needs of the people you encounter and guide you in praying about the situation. For example, pray for the homeless person on the corner that God would provide work, the basic necessities of life, motivation,

and so on. Pray for the mom screaming at her children in the parking lot that her stress level may be relieved and the children protected from evil. Pray for the teenagers who are smoking while walking home from school that they may embrace good habits and that their parents will encourage them in this time of transitioning self-esteem. Each of us has a story behind our behavior. Ask God to show you what to pray for, and then use whatever word or phrase comes to mind.

TEACHING THE DISCIPLINE

Once you have established your own rule of prayer, you can begin to help your children develop theirs. Make it simple and short, at least initially. Following are some examples of rules or routines that you could adapt to your situation.

EARLY CHILDHOOD *(ages 4–7):*

1. Have your children memorize a short prayer written by someone else for mealtime, such as the classic, "Come, Lord Jesus, be our guest. Let these gifts to us be blessed. Amen." Or ask one of your children to write a short prayer that the family will use at mealtime for a week. Say the prayer out loud together and follow it with a short time of silence in which anyone is free to add a spontaneous petition.

2. Have your children memorize a written prayer to say with you before they go to sleep. For example: "Now I lay me down to sleep, I pray the Lord my soul to keep. Watch over me throughout the night and wake me with the morning light." Then you

and your children can each pray spontaneous prayers asking for God's blessing on parents, grandparents, siblings, and so on before ending with the Lord's Prayer. Make this prayer-time ritual as important as brushing teeth and other bedtime routines. Consider doing this while kneeling beside the bed.

3. Teach your children about javelin prayers by praying "the beasts of the field and the birds of the air." Every time you see a creature, thank God aloud for creating it. Fill this prayer of gratitude with the awe it deserves.

MIDDLE CHILDHOOD (ages 8–11):

If you have not started a rule of prayer with your kids, use the "Early Childhood" ideas to help you develop one. In addition:

1. Create a prayer book for your family. Get a notebook and write down meaningful prayers that you or your children find in other sources. Also use it to write your own prayers in, much like the prayer journal described earlier in this chapter in the "Practicing the Discipline" section.

2. When traveling around town, have your children take turns doing a spontaneous prayer for a situation they see. Talk about body language and facial expressions and what that may tell them about how the person being prayed for is feeling inside.

3. Keep cards sent to you at Christmas or for other special occasions in a basket near your dining room table. Each day pull out one or two. Read the card out loud, and then pray for the people who sent it. This becomes a rule of prayer for the whole family.

ADOLESCENCE *(ages 12–15)*:

Help your teens develop a rule of prayer using words from other Christians as well as their own words. In addition:

1. Read aloud sections of *Prayer: Finding the Heart's True Home*, by Richard Foster. Commit to trying one type of prayer for a week, then another one for the next week, and so on. Set aside times when you can talk with your adolescent about that particular way of praying. Remember to be encouraging of their attempts. If something seems "weird" to them, don't push it. They may be more open to it later. You can decide whether to include children who fall into the middle age range (8–11) in this activity as well.

2. We can help adolescents become more comfortable with praying aloud in front of others by asking them to pray before the meal on occasion. The prayer could be extemporaneous or written out beforehand. Give your kids advance notice, but make the request special, as if an honor is being bestowed, which of course it is. The honor will be felt more keenly if it includes special holiday family dinners, such as for Easter or Thanksgiving.

3. Encourage young teens to join in the nighttime prayers with their younger siblings. Even though the prayers may seem "elementary" to them, it can be a comfort in the shifting sands of adolescence to pray in a way that goes back to early childhood. If you are just starting this idea with your adolescents, getting them to help with the rule of prayer for the younger

ones may be a way to get them hooked into the idea with less resistance.

THE BOTTOM LINE

Many of us plan "date nights" with our spouse or children. These are regularly scheduled times of being together. Ideally, those times strengthen relationships and are times we anticipate with joy. The goal is the same with a regularly scheduled prayer time with God. We seek joyful times of communication that strengthen our faith, though not all of our prayer "dates" will end with the feeling that that happened.

Remember, there is no wrong or right way to communicate with God as long as we are communicating as honestly as we can. Not all of us will move people to tears when we pray, but all of us will gladden the heart of the Father in heaven with our prayers. Commit to something this week that will deepen your conversation with God.

Chapter Three

THE DISCIPLINE OF FASTING

"When you fast, do not look somber as the hypocrites do, for they dis-
figure their faces to show [people] they are fasting. I tell you the truth,
they have received their reward in full. But when you fast, put oil on
your head and wash your face, so that it will not be obvious to [others]
that you are fasting, but only to your Father, who is unseen; and your
Father, who sees what is done in secret, will reward you."

MATTHEW 6:16-18

UNDERSTANDING THE DISCIPLINE

In the Discipline of Fasting, we deliberately deny ourselves an otherwise normal function of daily life for the sake of intense spiritual
activity. Through fasting, we learn that we truly do not live by
bread alone.

When Helen, who was not a practicing pastor of any sort, was
unexpectedly asked to deliver a simple homily over the graveside
casket of a good friend of the family, her mind froze. What message
of hope could she bring to others in the face of death's finality?
Being unaccustomed to speaking in public, how could she be sure
that her words would be the right ones? She had cared deeply
about the deceased—had often visited him at his sickbed—and
knew that those left behind needed to be comforted in their loss.
Was she up to doing it in a truly meaningful way?

During the few days she had for preparation before the brief graveside memorial service, Helen fasted, consuming only juice and water in the morning and eating a light protein-laced salad, followed by a broth similar to tomato soup for lunch and dinner. She refused all sugar products, breads, and heavy vegetables, such as potatoes. She asked God to honor each hunger pang as a way to grow closer to his heart and clarify the message he would have her deliver. She deliberately emptied her mind of anything but her ability to reflect God and the light of his love during the upcoming burial ceremony.

Fasting confirms our utter dependence upon God by finding in him a source of sustenance beyond food.

DALLAS WILLARD

Sharpening Our Spiritual Focus

There are hundreds of diet gurus out there, each one wanting our business, and when we gain weight, we choose from among their wares. While dieting, we fast for our physical well-being. In contrast, as Helen's story illustrates, biblical fasting hones our spiritual selves. We fast to sharpen our souls in much the same way that healthful dieting helps keep our bodies fit.

Fasting can increase our focus on God. If we are focusing on self—that is, fasting in order to force God to do something for us—we've missed the point and failed in fasting's intent. God will reward those who assiduously seek him, but that does not mean we can enact our will upon him through denial of food, as in "I've done this; I lived by this 'rule'; now God should do this other thing for me."

Nor is self-congratulation a part of fasting, as in thinking, *Look at me! Can you beat my piety? I fasted for a whole week.* Fasting is between God and the individual. It is not a public performance awaiting applause. Instead, it is a quiet event shared by only two. Fasting epitomizes the difference between looking at the sky with the naked eye and looking at it through a planetarium's telescope. When we give our attention to God through the powerful lens of fasting, distractions disappear and fuzziness becomes precision. We perceive more clearly the object at the center of our focus—God.

Our self-denial must first of all be humble. Otherwise it is a contradiction in terms. If we deny ourselves in order to think ourselves better than [others], our self-denial is only self-gratification.

THOMAS MERTON

The Holiness of Self-Denial and Abstinence

While biblical fasting calls for self-denial in order to sharpen our spiritual focus, it does not call us to become an ascetic. Ancient ascetics denied themselves virtually everything and added self-flag-ellation into the mix. They sought to suffer physically because of their lowliness in the face of God's majesty. Biblical fasting is quite different. It is unshowy, undemonstrative, and intended to increase our understanding that food comes in both physical and spiritual forms. Both types are nourishing. In fact, our lives depend on our ability to ingest each one.

We step onto holy ground when we seek to follow the path such people as Moses, David, Paul, and Jesus Christ have walked before us. Self-denial and abstinence help strip us of physical cravings and pleasures so that we more easily discern God's voice — though there is nothing easy about fasting. To fast is to humble ourselves. When we begin a fast, we discover very quickly how much of our daily life revolves around the thinking about, shopping for, and eating of food. It is not overstating it to say we crave food — certain kinds in particular — and continually look forward to our next meal. Eating our favorite things brings us instant gratification.

At times, many of us use food as a replacement for something else lacking in our lives, such as a happy marriage, good friends, or meaningful work. When we are stressed, many of us seek solace in what we call comfort food, failing to realize that we will never find in bags of our preferred groceries the calm center of God. We must eliminate whatever food crutch props us up if we cannot walk without it. We must cast it aside and actively ask God to enter our lives in place of it. We then can replace our physical dependence upon certain foods with a sumptuous spiritual feast.

---

*The way to avoid evil is not by maiming our passions,
but by compelling them to yield their vigor to our moral
nature. Thus they become, as in the ancient fable, the
harnessed steeds which bear the chariot of the sun.*

HENRY WARD BEECHER

Feasting upon God

When my (Marti's) son Marc married his Chinese bride, Yan, her family held what is traditional in her culture: a huge wedding feast befitting an emperor with steaming cauldrons of this and huge platters of that—more than anyone could eat in one sitting—to represent their matrimonial joy. It was a celebratory banquet that seemed never-ending. As the guests all sat at big round tables, trays of food already in front of them, a parade of waiters continually emerged from the kitchen with yet more serving dishes, course after course after course.

We bring that same celebratory spirit when we feast upon God. When we are not sated with food, every self-imposed tummy growl reminds us of why we are fasting and that God wants to fill our emptiness with his presence and grace. This new form of feasting—fasting from food so that we can better draw near to God—brings wonder, and from wonder comes joy. Wonder that our complex bodies, which God made, can forego food for a period of time without harm. Wonder at the overwhelming majesty of the gifts God has given us, such as the world with all its geographic diversity and each of our family members with their unique, God-given personalities. Wonder at his love, unconditionally given—love that never fails, not even when our imperfections and ugly moments of spiteful pettiness are fully on display.

To feast on God is to carry this astonishing but true revelation of him with us wherever we go.

[Fasting] is our way of saying "no" to the serpent
forever waiting in the wings.

RABBI SHLOMO RISKIN

PRACTICING THE DISCIPLINE

Be prepared for a shaky start. You may have many times of failure before you get the upper hand over a protesting stomach. Don't expect any immediate spiritual "highs" when you first begin to practice this discipline. This is the same as starting an exercise program after years of living as a couch potato. Just as you will not look as if you belong on the cover of a magazine after one day of walking, your one-on-one life with God will not grow deeper the first few times you fast. Fasting, perhaps more than any of the other disciplines, takes serious practice.

1. Start small and stick with it. Here is some sound advice to follow from our friend Richard Foster:

> Begin with a partial fast of twenty-four hours' duration; many have found lunch to be the best time. This would mean that you would not eat two meals. Fresh fruit juices are excellent. Attempt this once a week for several weeks. In the beginning you will be fascinated with the physical aspects, but the most important thing to monitor is the inner attitude of worship. Outwardly you will be performing the reg-

ular duties of your day, but inwardly you will be in prayer and adoration, song and worship. In a new way, cause every task of the day to be a sacred ministry to the Lord. . . . However mundane your duties, they are for you a sacrament. . . . Break your fast with a light meal of fresh fruits and vegetables and a good deal of inner rejoicing.

After two or three weeks, you are prepared to attempt a twenty-four-hour normal fast. Use only water but use healthy amounts of it. . . . You will probably feel some hunger pains or discomfort before the time is up. That is not real hunger; your stomach has been trained through years of conditioning to give signals of hunger at certain times of the day. In many ways your stomach is like a spoiled child, and spoiled children do not need indulgence, they need discipline. . . .

Having achieved several fasts with a degree of spiritual success, move on to a thirty-six-hour fast. With that accomplished, it is time to seek the Lord as to whether he wants you to go on a longer fast. Three to seven days is a good time period and will probably have a substantial impact on the course of your life.[1]

2. Look up in a Bible concordance every reference to food and fasting. Start with God's command in Genesis 3:6 and go through the book of Revelation's discussion of the Tree of Life

(Revelation 22:2). What can you discern from these passages about why the Bible strongly promotes God—not food—as the source of life? Look for examples of growing closer to God through fasting. Write a goal or two for yourself, based on these passages. For example: "I will fast this week in order to better pray for someone who is ill" (based on Psalm 35:13).

3. Consider reading Arthur Wallis's 1968 book *God's Chosen Fast* (Christian Literature Crusade, Box 1449, Fort Washington, PA 19034). Valerie has found this book to be personally useful and highly recommends it as "one of the best books on fasting available today."

4. Pay attention to the foods you turn to when you are feeling stressed, frustrated, or tired, and write them down in a journal. Pick one of those food items and start by doing a twenty-four-hour fast from it. You can expand the scope and time periods gradually over the next weeks. Each time you feel hungry for that particular food, ask God to satisfy your hunger and to provide the comfort that the food item previously did.

TEACHING THE DISCIPLINE

A word of caution: Children in our modern world face two food-related crises—the growing crisis of childhood obesity and the crisis of anorexia and bulimia among teenagers. These are huge worries.

Fasting from certain foods, especially those containing sugar, could help provide a healthy antidote for an overweight child, particularly if coupled with the encouragement to view God as life's sweetener. But if you have seriously skinny kids who nonetheless perceive themselves as fat, you are into an emotional realm that requires healing, and fasting is not the way to heal. Anorexic adolescents need professional counseling and a doctor's care. Until their mental and physical health is stabilized, we do not recommend practicing this discipline with underweight children. In general, even healthy children should not engage in total food fasts for more than one meal. They need the food for nutrition and proper development.

As you present this discipline to your kids, make it as appealing as possible in the beginning and start small. One of the great dangers of teaching children the disciplines, especially this one, is that we risk turning our kids off so completely that they will never again look at the spiritual disciplines as a blessing. Therefore, tread cautiously, prayerfully, and in great humility. Have some thought-out, structured fun time to replace the food being given up.

EARLY CHILDHOOD (ages 4–7):

1. Help your young children select any food containing refined sugar and give it up one day a week. The rule might be something like, "On Wednesday nights we don't eat cookies." Be sure to serve one of your kids' favorite meals on Wednesday nights. Let your kids know that Wednesday is God's night, that he becomes our dessert instead, and that time spent with him—and each other—is a treat to look forward to that is even better than dessert. At the end of your meal, sing songs together about God and thank him that he gave us musical

voices. Gradually work up to an entire day of fasting from refined sugar and then up to several days over a span of several weeks.

2. Encourage a healthy and positive attitude toward food. Present nutritious, attractive food, but don't become a restaurant. Do not refer to picky eating as "cute" or allow your children to have a long list of foods they won't eat. Explain that all food comes from God. Together, thank him for the food in front of you, specifically naming the food items on your children's plates in your before-dinner prayer.

3. This is more of a caution than an idea for teaching, but it's important enough to warrant a section of its own. Sometimes we parents inadvertently comfort our children's tears with food. We say something like, "It'll be okay, honey. Here, do you want a cookie?" This is a dangerous practice; in later years—including adulthood—treats can become a way to self-soothe anxiety that leads to obesity or, worse, a substitution for God himself. Instead of seeking God when we're sad, we go to the refrigerator or cookie jar as our solace because that's the pattern we picked up in our childhood. This is *not* a message any of us wants to send when our children are young and at their most impressionable stage. When occasions requiring comfort arise, hold your kids close and console them with the reassurance of your bigger, more powerful, and loving body, and then say something like, "Let's pray together that God will help you through the hurt."

As another part of teaching them to deal with food in

healthy ways, allow your children to stop eating when they are full. There is no healthy reason under the sun to insist on children eating until their plates are clean. "Starving people in China" are not going to gain any nourishment if you insist your kids eat until all food has disappeared and there is nothing more to eat. The only people you harm in that circumstance are your children. It can start a downward slide into obesity. Start encouraging healthy eating habits when your children are young, and consistently carry it through their childhood and adolescence.

4. Another part of starting kids on a healthy course in life is to encourage them to participate in physical activity and then energetically join them in play. At this age it can be tag, hide-and-seek, or any other common outdoor game favored during early childhood. Not everything can be turned into a spiritual lesson. What you want at this point is to set in motion healthy patterns of eating and exercise.

MIDDLE CHILDHOOD (ages 8–11):

Children in this age range have probably already developed some bad habits when it comes to food, and if fasting is a new concept for them, it will be more difficult for them to embrace than for younger-aged children. So think carefully about how you should present this idea and where to begin.

1. Start slowly. For instance, begin by eliminating dessert on Wednesdays and Fridays. Or perhaps fast from meat on those

days and eat vegetarian—but serve something appealing to
kids, such as macaroni and cheese or spaghetti with no meat in
the sauce. Don't use this time to introduce them to food that is
foreign to them.

2. On the nights when your family is practicing this discipline,
explain what you are doing. Introduce the word *sustenance* and
explain that it is a form of nourishment. It can come from
food, but that's not the only way to get it. Sustenance means
"to sustain life, to be provided for." Food comes from God—it
is provided by him—and that's why we say grace before a
meal. Offer an explanation such as, "Tonight God himself will
replace our dessert. Our dessert tonight will be a special prayer
to God for spiritual sustenance, that he will always be with us
to protect us from bad or scary things."

3. Fast from snacks one day a week or all weekend. Place Bible
verses on small cards and keep them in a container in your
kitchen. These are the rules of this game: When you feel the
need for a bite of a little something, draw one of these cards,
read the verse on it, thank God for speaking to you through
the Bible, and let that small taste of him be your snack.

4. Talk about specific language your children can use to refuse
something if they are offered it during a food fast. The rule of
hospitality always supercedes the law of fasting, meaning it is
better to eat a small amount of the dessert served at the friend's
home than to make a fuss about your fast. The goal isn't to
draw attention to yourself or embarrass your host.

If your children are invited to a birthday party on a traditional fast day, talk to them about how they should respond. Allow them to attend, guilt-free. We are not saved by what we do or do not eat; it is the motive for our fast that counts. Help your kids see that training in the spiritual life—especially where fasting is concerned—is just like training in the physical life when we have to practice a skill in order to become better at it.

ADOLESCENCE (ages 12–15):

1. Talk very frankly with your young teenagers about the image they have of their bodies. Puberty can be dreadful for some children. The weight gain that comes for many kids right before puberty starts keeps them healthy during this significant transition in their physical development. If your children are eating well and exercising regularly, the idea of their being "fat" should never cross your lips. However, the media will not help your cause. Much advertising aimed directly at teens will show very thin or very muscular people who are about eight to ten years ahead of them in the growth cycle. For girls, it is critical that their fathers respond well to them and for boys, their mothers. We must do all we can to balance the message of self-indulgence with solid, godly self-esteem. This task can be accomplished only through the grace of God and much prayer.

2. Caffeine is addictive. If you don't believe it, just talk to someone who has tried to kick the caffeine habit. (It took me six months, but I have successfully conquered it!) Many

adolescent kids have unwittingly become addicted to caffeine, primarily through the downing of Coca-Cola and Pepsi products, diet or otherwise. Work with your adolescent youngsters to give up all forms of soda pop—Mountain Dew is a terrible culprit because of its even higher caffeine concentration (don't think that all caffeine comes in "brown" forms)— and replace it with time in God's presence. Call it exactly that: "Time in God's presence, feasting on him while fasting from soda pop." As a substitute, buy a small book of daily prayers for your teens to read. Or take them on a drive to see something glorious in nature: the way snow drapes fir trees, crocuses budding from cold ground in the early spring, a field of native sunflowers, leaves changing color in the fall. Talk with them about what they learn about God from this time in his presence.

3. Throw a party that celebrates God, and don't have any food except fruit juice or a fresh-fruit punch. Play games and distribute party favors (hats that say, "We ♥ God," noisemakers, streamers, and the like). This celebration could be held near Thanksgiving or Christmas, on New Year's Eve, or on the Saturday before Easter. String a banner from your house that reads the same as the hats. Give out party favors: small Bibles or books of wisdom or prayer, plaques commemorating the Cross, or anything else of the kind.

Invite all members and guests of your church youth group. (Enlist your youth group leader in the planning.) Play games with God variations: Red Rover, Red Rover, Let God's Disciples

Come Over (each child wears the name of someone from the Bible on a "Miss America" style ribbon strung from shoulder to waist); basketball that spells out J-E-S-U-S rather than H-O-R-S-E; or Spin the Bottle for Jesus (when the bottle points to the person, he or she reads aloud a preselected verse from the Bible, and everyone cheers and whoops and hollers after the reading). When the partygoers leave, ask your teens if that wasn't one of the most fun parties they've ever attended. We expect they will answer you with a resounding "Yes!"

One caution here: Many adolescent children are in sixth, seventh, or eighth grade. This idea works best for that age group; high schoolers are likely to be a bit more skittish about it, perhaps viewing this type of party as too juvenile.

4. Prepare your evening meal as a family, especially if your entire family consists of teenagers—this can also be done as a Saturday or Sunday lunch—but instead of eating it yourselves, take your home-cooked food while it is still warm to a needy family or to elderly shut-ins. If possible, stay to serve the meal and clean up the remains afterward, storing leftovers in the refrigerator of those who accepted your gift. Stay to chat a bit and get to know those you served. When you return to your home, pray by name for the individuals who received your bounty. Discuss with your kids how our fasting from food that is normally abundant in our homes can on occasion be consecrated to others as a way for us to show the face of Christ to the less advantaged in our community.

THE BOTTOM LINE

By practicing the Discipline of Fasting, you and your children will reach true awareness of what it means that we do not live by bread alone. It is an essential step in the spiritual journey you undertake when you willingly seek a deeper relationship with your Lord and Creator, and it is that relationship that keeps you internally safe as you navigate your life's path.

Chapter Four

THE DISCIPLINE OF STUDY

Do your best to present yourself to God as one approved, a [person] who does not need to be ashamed and who correctly handles the word of truth.

2 TIMOTHY 2:15

UNDERSTANDING THE DISCIPLINE

In Romans 12:2, Paul tells us: "Do not conform any longer to the pattern of this world, but be transformed by the renewing of your mind. Then you will be able to test and approve what God's will is—his good, pleasing and perfect will." The Discipline of Study helps us "renew our minds" through intentional learning so that we have the mind of Christ, seeing people, situations, and events as God views them. In this discipline, we seek to become analytical and knowledgeable in our understanding of Scripture, current events, history, and relationships.

The "tapes" we play—those messages and ideas that we "hear" unconsciously day after day—strongly influence our actions and reactions. The goal in the Discipline of Study is to replace erroneous and destructive tapes with truths about God and the world he created: he is love, he cares for each one of us, *worth* is not the same as *usefulness*, and so on. As God renews our minds, we gain a larger perspective.

My (Valerie's) friend had a controlling, tyrannical father who used the Christian faith to support his behavior. When he died, he was disgusted that his children had not lived up to his expectations (though they were good kids who turned out to be responsible adults), so he left all his money to the church my friend attended. Through much prayer, talking with godly people, disciplining her feelings and responses, and working with a Christian counselor, my friend was able to have the mind of Christ in an unfair, hurtful situation. She trusted that God's hand had been at work in her father's life and was currently at work in her life and in her siblings' lives. This truth enabled her to acknowledge her feelings of hurt and not become bitter and resentful toward her father. This took time and intentionality. In order to be able to move forward in forgiveness and grace, my friend had to study who God is and how he views us. Her study of God transformed her mind.

Our Primary Focus

The Discipline of Study begins with our study of the Bible, our primary focus. While the Discipline of Meditation asks, "What does this mean *for me personally?*" the Discipline of Study asks, "What does this mean?" Meditation is subjective; study is objective.

Practicing this discipline is similar to reading a mystery novel. Avid mystery readers train themselves to look for clues, asking themselves, *Is this important?* They know that every detail and conversation counts. In the Discipline of Study, we analyze Scripture, asking ourselves, *What does this mean?* In our study of Scripture, we can read various commentaries to learn what people over the centuries have said about particular passages. We also read classical devotional literature, such as *Devotional Classics.*[1] We may enroll in a Bible class, take a seminary course, or use a study guide to help us better understand a particular book of the Bible.

To help ensure that we do not misuse or misunderstand what we are studying in Scripture, Dallas Willard offers the following insight:

> We will be spiritually safe in our use of the Bible if we follow a simple rule: *read in a repentant manner.* That is, read with readiness to surrender all we are, all of our plans, opinions, possessions, position. Study as intelligently as possible, with all available means, but never merely to find the truth and still less merely to prove anything. Subordinate your desire to find the truth, and your desire to have others do the truth, to your desire to *do it yourself!*[2]

If we study Scripture in this manner and within a faith community that values accountability, we can be more confident of our conclusions about who God is and how he works in the world.

There is a difference between memorizing Scripture and thinking biblically.

TIM HANSEL

Other Places to Look for Clues

We can also look for God in the world around us. He has planted evidence of himself in the natural world, and we can see him at work in history and current events as well as in people.

We apply this discipline when we intentionally seek to gain knowledge about the natural world. Our study then informs our conclusions. For instance, we may study books on the seasons and the rotation of the stars and see the evidence of order in the universe. As we ask ourselves, *What does this mean?* we could conclude that God likes order.

Or we might study a specific natural event, such as the eruption of Mount St. Helens. We might read and learn about what the mountain was like before and immediately after the blast, what scientists said about the resulting devastation, and what is happening on the mountain currently, all the while asking ourselves what this means. As we read about the plant and animal life that is returning to the mountain and then visit the mountain and see nature's regenerative aspects, we observe that nature reflects some of God's attributes.

By studying the natural world, we can conform our minds to the message God has left there, a message of truth and beauty.

God has provided us with many tools, in terms of people and their writings, that provide us with materials for genuine study. This discipline calls us to know the history of the church and the great thinkers of the church who have gone before us. To become more knowledgeable, we can read biographies of great Christians or the writings of Thomas Merton, Dietrich Bonhoeffer, St. John of the Cross, and others. Even novels can help us stretch our vision of what it means to be human and imperfectly live in a world where redemption is not only possible but is waiting for us. We might go to conferences or lectures. Marti once heard Corrie ten Boom speak of her concentration-camp experiences. Corrie mentioned how she and her sister, stark naked, carried a Bible into and out of the shower room, and no guard ever noticed—compelling eyewitness evidence of a God who lives with us in the here and now, all reasons and opportunities for further study.

In this discipline, we also intentionally look for God in history or current events. As we study current and past events using history books, news analyses, and discussion groups, we can observe some of the ways God may be working through an event. For example, the war with Iraq prompted me to study the Crusades, better understand the motives behind those "holy wars," and better develop the mind of Christ. As I began to see how the Crusaders believed they were doing the will of God, just as do some Muslims today who inflict violence on those whom they view as enemies of God, I began to pray for the Muslim people. I prayed for forgiveness for the damage done to people of all faiths in the Middle East by the Crusades and for God to heal those wounds. I prayed that the Muslim world might encounter the love of God and come to understand that it is love, not violence, that overcomes all evil. I prayed that the most recent conflict would not be viewed by the people of the Middle East as another Crusade.

Through the Discipline of Study, we train to be God's representatives to each person we encounter and in each situation we find ourselves. We study human behavior and personality theories so that we may ask what God might be doing in a specific individual or situation. We look for the emotions, experiences, and thoughts behind the actions so that we might better minister to people and pray for them. For instance, instead of getting irritated by our neighbor's constant rants about his wife and family, we prayerfully ask, *Why might this man be so unhappy? How might I get to know him better so that I can learn more of his story and as a result better pray for him and his family?* Or, when little Johnny goes ballistic when he thinks the lights are going to be turned off, thus leaving him in the dark, we ask, *Has this little boy been exposed to a real danger that he isn't able to talk about? How can I shine the light of Christ into his world? Do I need to investigate what may be going on in his home?*

When we prayerfully study ways to answer questions like these, our conclusions can draw us into a deeper relationship with Christ. Of course, we need to approach all of our conclusions with a spirit of humility, knowing that we will not assess every situation accurately. But as we fill our minds with Scripture and try to see the world through the eyes of Christ, we will find our minds more conformed to the image of Jesus. And from this intentional studying and focusing, as we come to better know God and his ways, we can, like Christ, give hope to the hopeless, spiritual sight to the blind, and a cup of cold water to those who are thirsty.

Remember, God wants to renew our minds so that we will better use them for his purposes. So if we ask for insight, God promises to give it to us. "If any of you lacks wisdom, he should ask God, who gives generously to all without finding fault, and it will be given to him" (James 1:5).

Set your minds on things above, not on earthly things.

COLOSSIANS 3:2

PRACTICING THE DISCIPLINE

Here are some ways to begin renewing your mind:

1. Join a structured Bible study that requires you to read Scripture every day, answer questions about it, and discuss the reading and your responses with others.

2. Join a book club or form one of your own with other avid readers. Read a portion every day from the next book you will be discussing. If you are new to this discipline, consider doing this with other Christians at first. Many pieces of classical literature, as well as contemporary novels, reveal divine truth in their honest depiction of human events and themes of reconciliation or redemption. Your goal is to learn to think biblically and apply it to all scenarios, fiction or real life. Learn to use anything you read, see, or hear to develop the habit of asking how God may be at work.

Here's an example of how one woman I know used the Discipline of Study. Several years ago she was talking with a woman who had just finished reading a novel about abuse. The woman told our friend that the abuse, though fictional, felt very real to her and had disturbed her. She also said she didn't quite know what to do with her sorrow. As she listened to this woman, our friend silently asked how God was at work in this woman's life through this piece of fiction and, as a result, suggested to the woman that she pray for people for whom the abuse was a reality.

3. Train yourself to listen deeper than words being said, to interpret body language. Try to hear the true message, even if it differs from what is being articulated. For instance, when your daughter comes home and says that she is sick of school, ask her specific questions to find out what is really going on inside her. Did she have a bad day? If so, why? Is she struggling with a particular person or with some subject matter? Is she being harassed in some way?

4. Sign up for a course offered online or at your local community college. It doesn't have to go toward a degree; it just needs to be a topic that intrigues you. Use it as a time to sharpen your critical thinking skills, an important tool in this discipline.

5. Spend a year learning about something. Read every book an author has written, taking notes on your reading. Choose a subject such as butterflies or biblical archeology or the book of Romans. Find books, articles, documentaries, and even experts in your area that can increase your understanding of that particular subject. Continually ask God to use what you learn to "renew" your mind.

6. As you read the newspaper, select one article or editorial opinion. Read it thoroughly and ask yourself: What or who is this article really about? What is biblically true about this article? What is blatantly false? How can I pray for this situation?

7. Take one relationship and try to better understand the other person. Find ways to ask that person about his or her background, hopes and dreams, and fears and failures. Think about how the pieces of information shared with you may have impacted the way that person lives today.

TEACHING THE DISCIPLINE

We must intentionally help our children process the world through God's eyes. Because a variety of things (friends, school, TV, movies, video games, Sunday school) give input into their minds and influence our kids, we must try to nurture godliness as much as we can. We also want to nurture strong study habits in our children because school is the focus of most of their daily life. Pray for opportunities to train your children in the Discipline of Study.

This discipline, in particular, has much room for ideas, and we have by no means presented an exhaustive list of ideas. Keep in mind—always—that you are your children's first and foremost teacher and that no one can have more of an influence over their study habits and their desire to learn than you can.

What we love we shall grow to resemble.

BERNARD OF CLAIRVEAUX

EARLY CHILDHOOD *(ages 4–7):*

Children in this age range, as they have been since the moment they were born, are learning creatures. That's what they do best.

They are learning lots of things, whether you formally teach them or not. What we want to do here is present some ideas for helping direct their learning, because it is already happening.

1. Watch TV and movies with your children. In every movie and TV program, along with the accompanying ads, subtle and not-so-subtle messages bombard them. Talk with your kids about what they are viewing to help them begin to discern reality from fiction or fantasy. For instance, in many cartoons the characters undergo acts of violence and yet walk away unscathed. If we help prepare our kids early on to think critically—to question what they are seeing or reading—it will come more easily as they reach adolescence and adulthood when the messages are much more subtle.

2. Read books aloud as a family, and then discuss what parts represent real life and what parts don't. For example, the book *Frog and Toad Are Friends* presents a great opportunity to point out that even though frogs and toads don't actually talk to each other, this book teaches principles that apply to all friendships. Ask questions that will help your children realize what the book says about the kind of friend they need to be.

   In addition, after you read the story, get your children to talk about the book. What might they be trying to tell you about themselves? When my oldest daughter was five, she went through a stage when dogs frightened her. Quite by accident, I checked out a library book about a little boy who had to walk by a scary dog each day. One day, in fear and desperation, he threw a ball at the dog. The dog picked it up, brought it back with tail wagging, and dropped it in anticipation of playing. It turned out the dog was not mean after all, just unknown to the boy. When I was reading this story to her, my daughter listened intently. When we finished, she let out a sigh of relief and wanted me to read it again. Afterward, we talked about the story and about her fear of dogs. This book helped her realize that dogs don't always bark because they are mean; sometimes they bark in greeting and anticipation of play. This understanding lessened my daughter's fear of dogs.

3. Help your children write a book of their own. Younger children may need to dictate the words so that you can write it for them. You can even type their words to make the book appear more official. Have your children illustrate the stories they write. Make it into a "real" book with a folded paper cover, a title page, an "about the author" page (perhaps enhanced with a school photo), and even a page with the copyright date and publisher's name (a combination of family names or a pet's name, for instance). Then watch them read and study their very own books! Trust us, it will be one of their favorites and could lead to a whole shelf of other books written by the budding authors you are raising in your home.

4. Nurture your kids' curiosity by helping them discover the wonders of God's creation. Find something to study, and talk with your kids about what it can teach us about God. Objects worth studying that can convey this message are feathers from a bird, broken bits of shell from the beach, and your children's own

fingernail and toenail clippings or hairs from their heads, especially if you have access to a microscope. Compare and contrast what is seen. For example, how is a hair from your head
similar to your children's, and how is it different? Then ask
your child to think about how people are different from God.

5. Check out books from the library that identify birds, butterflies, flowers, trees, animal tracks, and so on. Take the books
along on walks to learn more about what you are seeing. This
exercise can be done with older children as well.

Middle Childhood (*ages 8–11*):

1. Again, watch TV or movies with your children, discerning
truth from falsehood and reality from fantasy. This doesn't have
to be done formally; it can be a quick comment in response to
the value presented. Commercials present especially good
study material because they are short and often obvious in
their manipulative devices.

2. Get a children's mystery from the library. (Ask the librarian for
one that is age-appropriate.) Some classic examples are the
Encyclopedia Brown series, the Nancy Drew or Hardy Boys
series, The Boxcar Children series, and *Spider Web for Two*, by
Elizabeth Enright. Discuss what it means to look for clues
when figuring out puzzling situations.

3. Discuss a difficult neighbor or schoolmate with your children.
Help them see the issues behind the problematic behavior or
suggest possibilities if you don't know the circumstances. Do
this in the spirit of "putting the best construction on every-

thing" and not in a spirit of gossip. Tell your kids that, "People who are happy don't act that way [how the neighbor or schoolmate is acting]." Sometimes this phrase can help them begin to see the pain or loneliness concealed inside difficult people.

4. To help your kids think beyond what the culture says about Christmas, Easter, Thanksgiving, Halloween, and other holidays, get a book from the library on the history of holidays. Usually in books with earlier copyrights, the religious history of the holidays is unapologetically emphasized. Read about each holiday before it arrives, and discuss how it has changed from its original intent to a more contemporary interpretation.

5. Look at your kids' computer games and teach them the difference between reality and fantasy. Don't assume that children know. I remember reading a tragic story several years ago about a young boy who was surprised that another child he had shot didn't get up after being hit.

6. Before going on a trip, get age-appropriate books from the library and read about the places you will be visiting. Study the history of the people, events, and buildings; the geology of the land; the weather and climate of the area; the animals and plants—anything that will help your children better understand what they will be seeing and experiencing.

ADOLESCENCE (ages 12–15):

1. Many TV ads use sex to promote their products, so the possibilities for discussion are abundant. For example, ask your

teens if any of their friends dress, behave, or talk similarly to what was presented in the ad (or movie or TV program). Don't be afraid to ask hard questions or push their perceptions to the logical conclusion, but do it lovingly. Never belittle them for their responses. If their logic is faulty, ask yourself if you have been intentional in helping instill critical thinking in them. There is no perfect media form, and we can't expect to keep our kids sheltered away like hothouse tomatoes (those don't have much flavor anyway!). But neither should we say that anything goes.

2. Start a discussion at dinner about a current societal issue or concern. Ask your children what they have heard or seen on the subject and how this has affected them. You may be surprised by what they say. Don't let this turn into a heated argument. Instead, use this to model how all of us struggle with complex problems in a very diverse society. Ask your librarian for a book that you could read together as a family about the situation. Maybe there is a good documentary on the history of the issue that could give perspective to the current situation or a lecture at the library or local college you could attend together.

3. Use time in the car for discussions. Take advantage of the "captive" audience. On long trips, try reading a book to everyone. Both of us have spent hours reading books to our children on car trips. Laughing and crying, when it is shared together, can be as much an act of study as anything we would generally find more profound. This helps kids fall in love with reading

and increases the sophistication with which they channel their intelligence. They have to think on a subtler and usually higher level to understand most humor. And everyone shedding tears in the car over a sad part encourages kids to continue with a full range of emotions into adulthood.

4. Take all questions seriously, even if the subject is difficult or embarrassing for you. Talking about topics such as sex, drugs, and alcohol can be hard for adults, especially if the activity was prevalent in the adult's past. We must always tell the truth, though we don't always have to share every detail of what we did. Honesty and the wisdom gained in these areas can bring you respect and trust from your children.

5. As political elections approach, discuss candidates and issues as a family. Talk about for whom you are going to vote and why. When possible, watch debates between candidates or panel discussions on an issue the voters face. Show your kids that sometimes decisions have to be made between the lesser of two evils. Model good citizenship by voting at every primary, local, and national election. Teach your children that issues in society need a Christian worldview; even run for office yourself, if appropriate. By training children at a young age to be discerning and yet treating them with respect when they see an issue differently than we do, we can keep lines of communication open well into the later adolescent years and beyond.

THE BOTTOM LINE

God has left clues of his kingdom and work everywhere: in the Bible, in nature, in current and historical events, and in people. We should constantly study and observe, asking, *Where is God at work in this situation or person's life?* When we do that, we will begin to be more Christlike in our thinking and, therefore, better able to speak a word of wisdom into many situations.

Chapter Five

THE DISCIPLINE OF SIMPLICITY

Keep falsehood and lies far from me;
give me neither poverty nor riches, but give me only my daily bread.
Otherwise, I may have too much and disown you
and say, "Who is the LORD?"
Or I may become poor and steal,
and so dishonor the name of my God.

P R O V E R B S 3 0 : 8 - 9

UNDERSTANDING THE DISCIPLINE

The Discipline of Simplicity creates an inward reality that results in an outward lifestyle. By letting go of the multiple things that control our lives, particularly possessions and obligations, we liberate ourselves to draw nearer to God.

A few years ago, Fred and I (Marti) went to Africa to teach tribal bushmen in Ghana and Kenya who had converted to Christianity and wished to return to their own people as missionaries. Some of them were native to the countries in which we taught, but many were not. And those who were not native or were from remote areas of the country had little money for usual forms of transportation, such as automobiles or airplane tickets. Instead, they walked for many miles and several days, sometimes weeks (in the case of a student from Uganda who carried all his worldly possessions on his back), to reach the place where we were holding classes in either Accra or Nairobi.

Fred and I learned more in the two weeks we spent with these amazing students than they learned from us, despite the fact that they would tell you differently. (Don't believe them.) These people, scarred with tribal tattoos cut into their skin by knifepoint, were gentle and loving and carried with them an inward reality—a confident and secure trust in God—that we could only envy. Their lives were simple and unencumbered, and though it seemed to us that they wanted for much, they believed they wanted for nothing. Their entire desire in life was to serve others and help those others find happiness and contentment in a very simple and basic trust in the goodness of Jesus.

If you don't change your beliefs, your life will be like this forever.
Is this good news?

ROBERT ANTHONY

Uncluttering Our Lives

While it is true that the lives of these wonderful African graduate students were devoid of material clutter and that their spirits and connection with God were wholly intact, we do not have to become exactly like them to experience something similar. We do, however, need to recognize that material clutter—so omnipresent in Western culture—can lead to devastating spiritual clutter. We have only to look at the stress of credit card debt or the amount of time spent on reaching or maintaining the standard of living we covet, and the strain all this puts on marriages and other relationships, to realize that contrary to what marketing executives may tell us, it's not true that "the more we have, the better our lives." Valerie discovered this a few years ago, and her daughters were there to witness, and learn from, her literal "unearthing."

Valerie and her family live in a mountain cottage more than a hundred years old. It contains only twelve hundred square feet, including two bedrooms and one small bathroom with a shower, but no tub. The house has many positive qualities (location, location, location), but space is definitely not one of them. For the last seventeen years, her husband, John, has been remodeling their home. One of his projects was to build a storage-rich hutch and credenza in the kitchen. Valerie loves kitchen gadgets and cooking, and she knew she had to downsize, even with the additional space the new built-in gave her. Here's how Valerie felt about the experience:

> Six hours after I began the project, we'd filled five boxes to go to charity and had several more boxes headed for the trash. It was embarrassing, especially because our observant children were home. What kind of example was I to be hoarding all this stuff? I only hoped that getting rid of things I loved and had once thought necessary would demonstrate that the more belongings you have, the more complicated your life becomes. This point was driven home stronger because the fun activity we had planned to do as a family that day kept getting postponed as more and more things came out of those small cupboards, each item needing to be dealt with.

The Discipline of Simplicity helps us understand that "less is more" because when we have fewer possessions and activities to worry about and keep track of, we have more time to enjoy life and focus on our relationships with God and each other. When we live out this discipline, we take on obligations out of joy, not because we "have to." I had to learn this the hard way.

Several years ago, I realized I was doing too much and that, for my soul's sake, I needed to simplify my life. I was engaged in too many things that I had no particular fondness for doing but that made me "look good" to others. Dreadful as it is to uncover one's own character flaws, I recognized two in myself: first, my guilt complex if I said "no" (I grew up desiring to please others) and, second, love of the flattery when people tell me I'm indispensable. Seduction by one's own ego is a fearful thing.

I recognized that I needed to find and follow my own passion and not simply copy the obsessions of others, so I deliberately set a new course for my life. After serving for years in every civic, religious, or professional organization that claimed to need my active participation as committee chair, facilitator, coordinator, presiding officer, or board member, I began learning to say "no" and then to say it again (one "no" never works; someone always returns to persuade anew). I started to learn how to balance my life—God, family, a few close friends who feel like family, plus meaningful work—and was no longer held hostage by the need to do things for other people's approval. More to the point, I had more time to grow my soul again and renew the strength of my spiritual life.

We mostly spend [our] lives conjugating three verbs:
To Want, to Have, and to Do.

EVELYN UNDERHILL

Rediscovering the Gift of Time

Perhaps because too much of it is eaten up in the acquisition of yet more things, each of us tends to complain about our lack of time. When we say that we don't have enough time to do something, we are really saying the clock enslaves us. We have no free or unscheduled time and frantically rush from here to there to get everything done before we drop exhausted into bed at night. We can counteract this tendency by reminding ourselves that we each are given twenty-four hours a day—no more, no less—and that it is up to us to determine how we will use the same amount of time we share with everyone else on the planet.

Most people believe that "doing" contributes to a full life. The fact is, it does—and it doesn't. It depends on what we are doing. Basically, our day has four sections: morning, afternoon, evening, and night. Most of us spend this last section sleeping, and that cannot be impinged upon (though it often is). If we think we can get by on less than six hours of sleep, we delude ourselves. Research repeatedly tells us that we adults need a minimum of seven to nine hours of sleep each night to maintain health and retain peak brain function. That leaves us three wakeful periods of the day. When we simplify our commitments, we find that we have more time to spend doing the things that are life-giving to us.

I have often worked as an out-of-town consultant in educational arenas. A friend who did the same once taught me to base my fee on how many of my time periods get booked. I now charge a different fee for one or for two of the available time periods during my day and refuse to work more than two of them on any given day. That is, no one can book me for a morning workshop, an afternoon meeting, and an evening dinner/speaking engagement. One of those three time periods (morning, afternoon, or evening) must be kept sacrosanct and require nothing of me. I'll gladly do morning and afternoon, morning and evening, or afternoon and evening, but I will not allow myself to be booked all three periods on the same day.

I've learned that I require time to myself, each and every day, and that the only days I am fatigued and out of sorts are those when I don't get time to myself. Sometimes, though rarely, I use this time to nap, but on other days I use it to take a walk, look up Scripture, listen to music, read, write, and—always—pray.

The art of art, the glory of expression and the sunshine
of the light of letters, is simplicity.

WALT WHITMAN

Standing Unencumbered Before God

My experience with this two-time-periods-a-day maximum has taught me that I don't need to define my life by its externals or what looks good on a résumé. If we want to embrace this discipline fully, we need time—time that is free and unplanned—to appreciate stillness. We need moments of living inside ourselves and getting in touch with our own feelings so that there is no self-deceit or façade that fronts our actions or intentions and hides our real self from others or from ourselves. Practicing simplicity means realizing we do not need to be more than we are or to do something different from what we want to do. It enables us to stand unencumbered before God.

When we come naked before our Lord, he cloaks us in his divine mystery, a mystery that we could contemplate forever. We need time to reflect upon things about God that we can't know. We also need time to be awed and comforted by the facets of God's nature we are able to discern. If we place ourselves on the lifelong path of creating a low-maintenance way of being in the present moment, we will not be weighed down with places to be or things to do that prevent us from carving out contemplative moments and savoring the satisfied spirit so ready to surround us if only we slow down.

*You cannot glorify God better than by a
calm and joyous life.*

CHARLES SPURGEON

PRACTICING THE DISCIPLINE

Those of us living in the Western world may find practicing a simpler lifestyle a particularly big hurdle to jump. Our culture is fraught with "muchness and manyness," a phrase we often hear our friend Richard Foster use. We are weighed down by time demands that seem almost impossible for us to control. In other words, the Discipline of Simplicity may present you with a greater challenge than the other disciplines do. Face up to this challenge with eyes squarely open and don't be surprised—and don't give up!—when things get rough, as they inevitably will. Pray continually for the spiritual strength and the inner discipline to meet each difficulty that smacks down and shadows your path, remembering always that the liberation of simplicity is an end goal devoutly to be coveted.

1. Analyze your daily calendar to discover how much time you spend planning and carrying out activities. Be hard on yourself. How many "musts" do you really have? If your priorities are "God, family/friends, and meaningful work," such as mine are, think deeply about what daily, weekly, or monthly activities match those priorities. If you find that many activities in your life bear little resemblance to them, you may want to find ways to unclutter your schedule.

    Years ago, Valerie created a master calendar to assist her in organizing her schedule and keeping her family sane. You may find this exercise helpful too. For more information about how you can create your own master calendar, see page 199.

2. Over the next month on a week-by-week basis, eliminate any extraneous activities from your calendar so you can begin to enjoy life and your family again. You might even want to go cold turkey for a month, meaning that you will refrain from

participating in anything but church, home life, and (if relevant) work for the next thirty days or so. As you reevaluate your social commitments and volunteer jobs, keep only the ones that feed you in the season of life in which you currently find yourself. Do not hold on to anything that saps you.

Remind yourself often that Jesus walked away from needs here on earth so that he could spend time in prayer and refreshment with his Father. We certainly can't and won't do a better job than he did, yet still we run ourselves ragged trying. Talk about ego! Try getting to the point where you can honestly say that you're not too busy and then *don't* take on anything more. Instead, spend that time doing things that nourish your soul and give you joy.

3. Learn to say "no." Here are some pointers:

- *Never* immediately say "yes" to a request to do something; *always* tell the person you will get back to him or her. This buys you time to think rather than commit. Live in faith that if you can't do the activity now (and would like to) that you will be able to later. Thank God for the season of life you are in at this moment, embrace it fully, and know that in a few years much will be different.

- If you don't like the activity you're being asked to take on, don't agree to it out of guilt. If you're asked to do something you dread, find a way to be honest. Unless it's part of a bigger commitment, such as your children being in a cooperative preschool with parents having to help out x-number of times a semester, don't ever say "yes" to things that don't refresh

you. God may have in mind someone else who is too shy to
step up without some coaxing. If you cave in with your
"yes," that person may not gain the opportunity to take the
reins. Whenever you do say "no," pray that God will bring
the right person in at the right time to fill the need.

• If you made a commitment that is not right, admit your error
immediately. Yes, you'll be embarrassed. Yes, the group will
be frustrated with you. Yes, you may not be asked to do
something else with that group. But if you can live with those
more than the stress of commitment, then by all means get
out of it now. Learn from the experience and don't put yourself in that position again.

• If you can't get out of the commitment, don't say "yes" to
anything else until you can extract yourself from it. Pray for
wisdom in completing the task as quickly as possible and for
insight in understanding how you got yourself there in the
first place.

• You don't have to share why you are saying "no." This is a
radical thought to some people. It's okay to say that this is
not the right time and leave it at that.

4. Simplify your possessions. Clean out your closets. When you
come home from shopping, exchange the new garment for an
old one that can go to charity. Find ways to participate in activities without spending money or needing specialized equip-
ment. For example, instead of joining a gym, take a brisk
half-hour walk around the neighborhood.

5. Refuse to undertake any new activity or to make nonessential

purchases until your current calendar, finances, and storage situation are under control.

6. Commit, if you haven't already, to recycling cans, newspapers, and anything else that can be used again by you or others. You will be pleased by how recycling releases you, via self-empowerment, from helpless worry about the mountain of garbage all of us are contributing to the world's ecosystem, which of course is God's creation, the same one of which he called us to be stewards (see Genesis 1:28-30). If we didn't have so much disposable stuff to begin with, nature would be better protected—that's for sure!

7. Remove the language of busyness from your conversations. Refuse to say, "I'm so busy." Get to the point where you can honestly say that you are enjoying a rich life. Find a new way to talk about the fullness of life that communicates pleasure, not dread, in your activities. Note how many times others mention busyness as an assumed way of living. Do they sound happy? Strive to be a witness to joy and enthusiasm in all of your conversations.

TEACHING THE DISCIPLINE

As parents, we want our children to hold every advantage in the world and to experience all kinds of activities and social interactions. We want them to have fun and be happy. While the Discipline of Simplicity embraces helping children develop interests and talents, it does not elevate such opportunities to the status of idolatry, to the point where we put doing and acquiring—keeping up with the family next door and friends at school—above growing a soul.

Remember, your kids will learn this discipline best from what you demonstrate, not from what you say. First comes *your* response to the discipline and then comes your children's.

EARLY CHILDHOOD (*ages 4–7*):

1. Help your children eliminate clutter in their personal spaces. This can be an overwhelming task—for anyone. Spend time going through all of their belongings with them. Help them see how having too many possessions can make life burdensome. When we keep our closets and drawers cleaned out, we can access them more easily. When we keep our things organized, we save time in locating what we want. With fewer toys and games and fewer committed activities, there's less possibility for sensory overload. With your children, give all the discarded possessions to a children's charity.

2. Keep the cleanout process going. Have an annual or semiannual "unclogging." It's difficult to stay ahead of the clutter without scheduling regular times to unclutter—for instance, on birthdays and again six months later. As mentioned before, give all the discarded possessions to a children's charity.

3. Help your children obtain their own library cards. Instead of buying books and other materials (such as videos or CDs), teach your children to borrow them and to take care of them so that others can also enjoy them. Teach them punctuality in returning these items. Encourage them to put the titles of books they would like to own on a list for possible birthday or Christmas

gifts. Or help them create their own books, which can be bound in a simple manner to keep on their personal bookshelves.

MIDDLE CHILDHOOD (ages 8–11):

1. Find out how your children *really* feel about all of their activities. Maybe there's something they're doing for your sake rather than their own. Be open-minded if they want to give up something that's near and dear to you. They may not be gifted in the same way you are, and you don't want to force your leftover dreams on them. At the very first opportunity, eliminate any activities your kids don't feel passionate about.

    For some kids accustomed to being scheduled every minute of every day, downtime will take some getting used to. Eventually, they'll either come to appreciate it, or they'll discover they really do want more activity in their lives. Everyone has a different level of need, and it will take some experimentation to find the right balance.

2. Let your youngsters help you hold a garage sale. Price their belongings (and yours) low so that they will sell. Your children can function as cashiers. Let them keep a commission on what they sell—say, 10 percent of the overall revenue—and then divide the rest between your church and a charity you mutually decide would benefit other children, such as the Make-a-Wish Foundation, the Leukemia and Lymphoma Society, or the Ronald McDonald House. Again, linking such giving to the discipline you are teaching helps children understand the spiritual foundation that upholds the need for the discipline.

3. If you are in a community where each birthday party has to be bigger and splashier than the previous one, call a halt to it right now. Return to the simpler times of your own childhood. What are your favorite birthday memories from the ages your children are now? Maybe those memories include the simplicity of holding an old-fashioned ice cream social. Have kids play in the backyard, doing silly stuff like running with a partner while holding an orange between their chins or running three-legged races. Let them make their own ice cream sundaes from a variety of toppings. Parents can dress in striped shirts with garters on the sleeves to add to the ambience.

4. Help your children learn now to conserve the world's finite resources. Take them on an outing to the city dump and discuss how much trash gets eliminated from every house every day. Ask them where they think all the throwaways go. Begin a recycling program in your home and expand it to your neighborhood. If your community does not already have a recycling program, take your kids to city council meetings and lobby for one.

ADOLESCENCE *(ages 12–15):*

1. Help adolescents go through their closets and drawers and pull out everything they haven't worn or used during the past year. If they aren't sure they want to part with a clothing item, have them turn its hanger around as they hang it back up. In six months, if the hanger is still backward on the rod, they will have a better sense of how important it really is to

them. In the case of other possessions, have them fill a box to be put away and reevaluated in six months. At the end of the six-month evaluation period, take all unused items to a charitable organization that will distribute them to those less fortunate.

2. Have a heart-to-heart conversation with your kids to determine which activities really interest them. Help them understand that doing something because they always have or because others do increases pressure on time and psyche. Teenagers actually require more sleep than they did in middle childhood because of the physical changes they're going through. If cutting out an activity can buy more downtime, their mental and physical health will improve. Plus, they will be more open to spiritual guidance.

3. Provide your teens with a financial budget for special events or occasions, and allow them to spend within that limit but not over it. When I turned sixteen, I asked that both my parents and grandparents give me money for my birthday so I could redecorate my room and rid myself of its childish touches. I didn't collect a huge sum of money, but my father agreed to provide labor for free (hanging the wallpaper and creating a wooden valance above my curtains). Still, all the materials had to come from my budget. It taught me about frugality and how to create something nice from very simple, inexpensive supplies.

THE BOTTOM LINE

The Discipline of Simplicity can lead to an uncluttered life, a life free from physical and metaphysical tyranny. By practicing this discipline, you will rediscover an abundance of time given to you by God for meaningful relationships with others, including one with him.

Chapter Six

THE DISCIPLINE OF SOLITUDE

Then, because so many people were coming and going that they
did not even have a chance to eat, [Jesus] said to them, "Come
with me by yourselves to a quiet place and get some rest."

MARK 6:31

UNDERSTANDING THE DISCIPLINE

A few years ago my husband and I (Valerie) took our girls to the
mountains for a day of snow tubing. We rented inner tubes and
made a run or two, enjoying the ride back up the rope tow. Then
into that pristine setting, rock-and-roll music, enhanced by a loud
speaker, shattered the peace. I pled with the guy behind the desk
to turn the music down, but he only laughed nervously with a
semibewildered look on his face. No one had ever made such a
request of him before, and he was confused and embarrassed. I
guess he assumed that earsplitting music was part of an outdoor
experience! I wanted to enjoy God's creation and the quiet, but the
music was so loud it distracted me from the beauty of the place.

No matter where we go, noise bombards us. It's with us at stop-
lights where radios blare from other cars. When someone puts us
on hold on the phone, we hear music or advertisements.
Unfortunately, some of us have grown so accustomed to constant
sound that we can't stand silence. As soon as we walk into a room,

we turn on the TV or radio for some "background noise." But with clatter filling all corners of our lives, it can be hard for us to focus our thoughts on our omnipresent God throughout the day.

This discipline is not *just* about being alone, for we can be alone and still have the distractions of external and internal noise. The goal of this discipline is to quiet our hearts and minds so that God can fill the silence.

Solitude doesn't help us recharge our batteries for the
rat race; it teaches us to ignore the rat race.

RICHARD FOSTER

Turning Off the Outer Noise

God rarely speaks above our noise. If you sometimes feel that God doesn't answer your prayers, check the amount of sound and distraction in your life. Perhaps you can't hear God speaking over the racket. As the prophet Elijah did, you may discover that God is not in the noise and fireworks but in a still small voice (see 1 Kings 19:9-13).

During a time of struggle with issues of faith, I decided to take a solitary retreat. A friend generously loaned me the use of her cabin in the mountains for three days. I read my Bible and other devotional materials, prayed, hiked, and wrote in a journal. Those three days of solitude and silence helped me get to the bottom of what I was feeling. No longer distracted by noise and activity, I came face to face with my fears and inability to trust in God, and I felt his presence intensely. Out of that time came a turning point in my faith journey that, over the years, has resulted in a greater boldness of witness and a deeper desire for the things of God's kingdom.

Stop reading right now. What do you hear? Where is it coming from? Is it necessary? If we aren't careful, sound can become an addiction—something we crave like alcohol or sugar.

Just as the body takes time to recover from an infection that has afflicted it, so the soul needs times of silence and solitude for its recovery from the insane pace of modern life.

HOWARD BAKER

Even Christian radio can be a distraction from hearing God. While Christian programs may teach us about God, they will, for the most part, do little to help us know God personally. Besides, not everything that comes over Christian radio stations is good or true. We need to be just as discerning about what we let slip in the back door of our minds and hearts through the Christian media as through the secular media. But this discipline is much more than simply eliminating outer noise.

Turning Off the Inner Noise

Most of us find it fairly easy to eliminate external noise, as we can turn off the TV or radio or stereo. If we live in a noisy neighborhood, we can find a quiet place in a library or church where we can listen to what God wants to say to us. But we find it much more difficult to quiet our minds.

Often when we have no noise around us, our minds start racing. We think about all the things on our to-do list, or we remember we forgot to mail Aunt Mabel's birthday card. The silence may make us feel nervous and anxious. Every bump and thump may cause us to worry, wondering what caused the sound.

For centuries, Christians have been training their minds in quietness by using the "Jesus Prayer." *Lord Jesus Christ, Son of God, have mercy on me, a sinner.* By saying this prayer over and over, we can "outshout the enemy." All those thoughts and worries that would distract us from sensing God's presence will flee at the name of Jesus. As we discipline ourselves to repeat the Jesus Prayer over and over, a sense of God-with-us begins to calm our minds and descend into our hearts.

I've often used this prayer to quiet my mind before entering—or even during—a challenging conversation or situation. Instead of worrying about what to say, I pray these words over and over, and it brings me a deep sense of peace and serenity. This deep peace is the ultimate goal of this discipline.

When we start being too impressed by the results of our work, we slowly come to the erroneous conviction that life is one large scoreboard where someone is listing the points to measure our worth. . . . In solitude we become aware that our worth is not the same as our usefulness.

HENRI NOUWEN

A Solid Core

The Discipline of Solitude encourages us to have regular times of external and internal quiet and stillness so that we can hear God speak to us. This discipline produces a solid, calm center out of which we can learn to speak an appropriate word to others, another goal of this discipline. Silence and stillness allow us to hear God's voice so that he can help us know how to speak to those we come in contact with. He may give us just the right words to say to a hurting neighbor, or he may reveal that we shouldn't say anything because the person isn't ready to hear or we're not as compassionate as we need to be. We may even hear that we need to apologize for how we have contributed in some way to the hurt or suffering.

The Discipline of Solitude invites us to empty our lives and minds of constant noise and clutter so that we may be filled with the still small voice of God and that from hearing God's voice we can speak to a hurting world.

When we get lost on the inside, most of us start to
panic. We wander from relationship to relationship,
from activity to activity, from distraction to distraction
in an attempt to find our way.
Perhaps what we need to do is just sit down.
There is an acronym in survival literature that says
STOP:
Stop. Think. Observe. Prepare.
Perhaps when we get lost on the inside, we need to use

the acronym for a slightly different slogan:
Surrender. Trust. Obey. Pray.

TIM HANSEL

PRACTICING THE DISCIPLINE

We need to train in this discipline because we live in a culture addicted to noise. We won't become comfortable with silence and solitude overnight, but we can set aside a bit of time each day to work on it.

1. As you seek to incorporate this discipline into your life, pay attention to what you do when your world becomes quiet. Do you welcome the time of silence, or do you immediately seek to fill the void with music or TV? Do a "noise diary" for a day. Write down the number of minutes a radio, TV, or stereo system is on. Include the number of minutes you spend talking. Was there more noise than you expected? Less?

2. Carve out some times of silence each day, whether at home, in your car, or at your place of business. Consider leaving the radio off in the car in the morning as you drive to work. Close your eyes. Become aware of what you hear: birds, traffic, dogs barking, the refrigerator humming. Listen for what God may be saying to you.

3. Set aside twenty-four hours to fast from the radio, TV, stereo, and all background noise, if possible. Record your responses in a journal. Consider committing to practice a once-a-week "noise" fast.

4. If you have trouble quieting your mind, use the Jesus Prayer: *Lord Jesus Christ, Son of God, have mercy on me, a sinner.* Say this prayer over and over, not as a magical formula but so that at the name of Jesus, every knee shall bow and every noisy spirit flee. It works. Next time you want to hear God and can't seem to, try it.

5. If we are used to noise all of the time, many of us will even try to fill in silences in conversations with random talking. Train yourself to say what you want to say and then stop. If the other person doesn't immediately jump in or even interrupt us before we are finished, often we'll continue babbling on until that person indicates that he or she will speak if we will be quiet.

6. Whenever possible, don't do another activity while simultaneously talking on the telephone. Focus on hearing what the caller is saying, and listen to what God is nudging you to say to the caller.

TEACHING THE DISCIPLINE

Noise is so ever-present in our culture that we don't even notice it until we intentionally turn it off. As you contemplate your goals in teaching this discipline to your children, try to assess how much noise is in their lives now and what an acceptable goal may be. For example, if your family always has the radio or television on when someone is home, begin by insisting that the family have thirty minutes of silence each day. As your family becomes more accustomed to silence, increase the length of time.

We want our children to have times of silence (externally and internally) so that they can hear God speaking to them. We need to help them create those silent spaces in their external environment and in their minds, but we also need to help them go to the next step of inviting God to fill that silence.

EARLY CHILDHOOD *(ages 4–7)*:

1. Occasionally, when you are driving in the car, play the "Quiet Game." Tell children that the winner of this game is the person who doesn't talk until you get to your destination (which should be no more than five minutes away). Not talking teaches young children a rhythm of engagement and withdrawal.

2. Have a thirty-minute period of quiet or rest at the same time every day, such as after school when your children have reconnected with you and have had a snack, or right after lunch. Allow them to quietly read but not watch videos or TV.

3. If your children are away from you during the day, use the time when you first see them again as catch-up time. Resist doing household tasks during the first half-hour you are with your children. Listen very attentively and concentrate only on them and what they have to tell you about their day. Not only will this be a powerful model, it will show your kids how important they are to you. This also models a rhythm of engagement and withdrawal. If they can count on that time of focused attention at home with you, they will more likely understand the need for you to focus on something other than them for a period of time.

4. At bedtime, have a time of silence during the prayers. Help

your children ask God to speak to them, and then have a short time of active listening. At the end of the prayer time, talk about any thoughts your kids may have had during that quiet time. If they fall asleep during the silence, rejoice that it was while listening to God.

MIDDLE CHILDHOOD (ages 8–11):

1. Again, work toward a daily time of quiet, and when you are talking with your kids about their day, stop doing other things and give them your focused attention.

2. Teach your children the Jesus Prayer, mentioned earlier in this chapter. Help them to realize it can be a comfort to them when they feel frightened, uncomfortable, or confused.

3. Try a time of silence during bedtime prayers with your kids. Help them to understand that like any conversation, prayer includes talking to God and listening to God respond.

4. Insist that your children turn off the TV when doing their homework. Watching TV and doing homework are two activities that are mutually exclusive—one requires total engagement (homework) and the other is a passive, slow-the-brain-down, very disengaged activity (TV watching). Television, by its low cognitive demand and its power to mesmerize, will interfere with homework in a way you perhaps never expected: it will help turn your kids' brains off—literally. Conversation, reading, and writing never do this, but TV does. Talk with your kids about the art and skill of concentration and of deriving energy from one's own willpower.

5. If your children are used to studying with music on, work out a compromise. For example, tell them that music can be on if they are coloring a geography map but that it must be off when they are doing their math or English assignment. In other words, wean them gradually.

6. Don't allow your children to ride their bikes or walk around outside with earphones on. Besides the obvious problem of not being able to hear approaching cars or other dangers, children who constantly wear earphones never learn to listen to what is around them because they have learned to tune out everything around them, including you. If they are used to tuning us as parents out, could they also be tuning out God's voice?

ADOLESCENCE *(ages 12–15)*:

1. Through the Discipline of Solitude, we seek to become more aware of what and who we are listening to. To train teens in this, set aside time to listen to their choice of music and discuss it with them. Be careful not to rant and rave about the music's words and style. Instead, try to hear what the song is saying, both through the music as well as the words. At the end of the song, instead of making statements, ask questions such as: What in the music appeals to you? A particular guitar passage, or the way the melody transitions at the end of the verse into the chorus? What do you think the words of the song are about? Have you experienced something similar? Your local bookstore or librarian can guide you to current

resources that more thoroughly explore discussing music with your teenagers.

2. Again, try to wean your teens from the habit of studying with music or the TV constantly on as background noise.

3. Encourage adolescents to leave their Walkmans at home periodically and to pay attention to the natural sounds around them. When you are traveling in the car, especially on family vacations, carve out some Walkman-free time so you can converse as a family, discussing where you are and what you are experiencing. Devote twenty minutes of every hour in the car to conversation.

4. Work with your young teens to have a daily time of solitude and quiet solely for the purpose of listening to God. It could be part of a Bible-reading time, during bedtime prayers, or right after dinner before doing homework. Talk with your teens about inviting God to speak to them. They could use Samuel's prayer from 1 Samuel 3:9: "Speak, Lord, for your servant is listening." Encourage teens to write in a "Solitude Notebook" what they feel God is saying to them, and then talk with them about it. Like all of us, teens need a strong faith community to help them discern the true voice of our Good Shepherd. If they are reticent to share these thoughts with you, encourage them to talk with a solid youth group leader or pastor at your church about what they feel God is telling them.

THE BOTTOM LINE

At the pace many of us live, we desperately need to hear Jesus call us to come away and rest, to withdraw from the fever and pitch of our lives and to refresh and restore ourselves in the Spirit of Christ. We need a quiet environment to let our minds rest, and we need quiet minds to let our souls rest in God. As we learn to practice this discipline, we become better at speaking words of comfort and direction to the people around us. We discover that silence is not empty when God fills it.

Chapter Seven

THE DISCIPLINE OF SUBMISSION

Submit to one another out of reverence for Christ.

EPHESIANS 5:21

UNDERSTANDING THE DISCIPLINE

As the oldest child in a family with a physically disabled father, my (Marti's) husband grew up as the little man of the house. His mother was at work all day, frequently leaving Fred in charge of his younger brother and sister. When he reached adulthood and married me, he continued to give orders. As you can imagine, I did not much like being ordered around or treated like a child. Fred, on the other hand, never saw always taking charge as a flaw. His presumptive bossiness, learned in childhood as a survival trait, threatened to divide us as a couple, but neither of us really knew what to do about this part of his ingrained personality. In all other ways, he was a very loving man.

On one of Fred's birthdays, I planned a surprise getaway for him. I packed an overnight bag for both of us, went to his place of work on a Friday afternoon, and kidnapped him. Two coconspirators were already in the car with the engine running. Fred was whisked inside the waiting vehicle and transported away. We had a fabulous weekend, and Fred hadn't had any say in it. The experience helped show him that submitting to others sometimes pays off in remarkably liberating ways. His only task was to sit back and enjoy the ride, which he found an incredible relief in his stressed out, decision-burdened life.

The Discipline of Submission liberates us from the burden of needing to get our own way or the monumental mental exertion of constantly having to be the authority on everything. While some may balk at the idea of giving our will over to someone else, this discipline offers joy and freedom, with the side benefit of improving our relationships with others. It also helps lead us toward humility, an essential spiritual trait.

Subordination Versus Submission

Submission and *subordination* are most definitely not synonymous terms. To be subordinate to another is to have no say. To be submissive to another is *to choose* to have no say, a distinct difference.

The great militaries of the world have always used subordination as a way to keep order in the ranks, with strict reprisals if the chain of command is not respected. People have been severely punished—court-martialed, thrown in the brig, or otherwise disciplined—for not paying enough attention to the military pecking order or for daring to question a superior officer. The very term *superior officer* symbolizes one person's inferiority as compared to another's superiority. In wartime this works; in family life it is spiritually destructive. Consequently, we usually bristle when someone demands subordination from us. We want to choose submission and not be coerced into it.

Submission represents freedom of choice, a much healthier

way to approach mutually beneficial relationships. We can opt for submission through our own internal resolve. No one imposes submission upon us; we elect it. It's our own free will that determines to whom we will be submissive and on which issues. And because it connects us to others, whereas subordination disconnects us from others, submission ultimately liberates us.

Practicing the Discipline of Submission means willingly choosing to let another person take the lead. We do this as training for our own submission to God. It helps remind us that we are not in charge—God is.

Submission in an earthly sense means gladly giving up some or all of our own control over people and events so that others may benefit. For instance, I always submit to Fred driving our car, and not because it is a cultural norm for men to drive. The fact is, Fred likes to drive, and it is a small pleasure I can do without. Another woman I know submits to her husband in the kitchen. He loves to cook and does it well, and she concedes the kitchen to him as his domain instead of hers. A husband I know submits his social calendar to his wife. He has learned to relax and have fun with whatever entertainment arrangements she makes for them on the weekend. She submits by sometimes incorporating sporting events into those plans, knowing that he likes them.

There is no happiness where there is no wisdom;
no happiness but in submission.
SOPHOCLES

Recognition of Submission's Limitations

Subordination and submission do have one thing in common: They each can help us pander to an all-too-human desire to become infantile again. Often when prisoners are released, they don't know how to live in a world where they are not fed, housed, and clothed on a daily basis. They have not had to make any livelihood decisions for many years. And people who willingly and regularly turn every daily decision over to someone else—through self-selected submission to another—can embrace their childhood again. This is not healthy behavior. Nothing taken to an extreme usually is.

In pursuing the Discipline of Submission, we should never lose our own sense of personhood. God created us as unique, creative individuals, unlike anyone else anywhere at any time. He certainly does not intend for us to be subsumed by the force of another human being who is as mortal and fallible as we are. Instead, he commissions us to act upon the gifts with which we have been bestowed and to be in personal relationship with him, the One who created us. If we willingly give all of that away to someone else to decide and do for us, we are liable to become invisible to ourselves and erode, if not lose, our own private connection to God. This discipline has nothing to do with our becoming doormats with no will or mind of our own. We are to be neither self-hating nor arrogant.

Humility is the opposite of self-deprecation. It is the grateful recognition that we are precious in God's eyes and that all we are is pure gift.

HENRI NOUWEN

Rejoicing in Submission's Power to Free Us

The Discipline of Submission reminds us to cease trying to control other people or the circumstances around us. Through submission, we accord other people the right to their own free will and the use of their own independent minds. Their dreams and plans become important to us. This discipline frees us from the bondage of irritation if people don't treat us a certain way. We no longer have to stew if some event didn't go exactly as we planned. We can rejoice with others' successes without trying to one-up them with a success story of our own. As Richard Foster writes, "We discover that it is far better to serve our neighbor than have our own way."[1]

Mutual submission with others enables us to become more, not less. The whole is truly greater than the sum of its parts. No one was stronger or more submissive than Jesus. As God, he could have walked away from everything bad that happened to him, but he chose to submit his will to his Father's will. Through that strength and submission, he became the Great Liberator. No one who trusts Jesus can deny the freedom there is in him.

Submission is an act of giving that, like most such acts, results in receiving blessings we cannot even begin to anticipate. God asks us to practice submission so that we may be in concert with him, and he rewards lavishly when we accede to his will.

---

*Sow an act and you reap a habit; sow a habit and you
reap a character; sow a character and you reap a destiny.*

Frances E. Willard

Practicing the Discipline

As individual human beings, male or female, each of us generally likes to be the one in charge. We like to be listened to, and we resent it if people ignore us. Indeed, we glory in our independence, not unlike teenagers who are going through that necessary identity separation phase of their lives. Sadly, not all of us outgrow it. Don't berate yourself if you are one of those people; just commit to learning how to become more submissive.

1. Start with the little things of everyday life. Look for ways you can give up your own desires or convenience for the sake of the greater good. For example, the next time you go grocery shopping, return your cart to the designated parking lot corral, even if it is inconvenient. This small courtesy prevents vehicles from being blocked or, worse, having loose carts slam into them. Or slow yourself down and hold doors to public places open for people you don't know, and smile and greet them. When other drivers try to merge into traffic, move to the left lane and let them in. Little acts of submission and service such as these test how deep are our integrity and reliance upon this discipline.

2. Observe your voice tone and actions when dealing with people. Write down what you observe. Are you disciplining your children with love, or in anger? Are you being harsher than necessary with a slow waitress or a mix-up in your order at a restaurant? (Being strict and firm does not necessarily imply irritation and yelling.) Ask a trusted friend or spouse to give you candid feedback about how you treat others. Don't feel

resentful if the feedback isn't as flattering as you'd like.

Consider what you've been told and be grateful that someone has been honest enough with you to help you change.
Become mindful of all that you say and do in respect to other
people so that you can rub out old patterns and establish new
ones. Allow yourself to fail from time to time; forgive yourself
and move on. But always be aware that you are getting rid of
the rags in your life and instead clothing yourself in God's garments, the ones he prefers for you to wear. Resist turning those
new garments into old ones.

3. Become aware of how you respond when you suffer an injustice from another person. If you respond in an arrogant way,
immediately apologize, if possible, and give yourself the same
grace to be human that God gives you. No one is perfect; we
all have bad days. But we need to be more aware of situations
that trigger in us a nasty, biting response.

4. Kids are great observers but poor interpreters. Even when they
outwardly appear to be engrossed in something, they can
inwardly be picking up every word and nonverbal reaction
going on around them. Think about what your children are
observing about you. Do they see you playing by jungle rules
(survival of the fittest), or by kingdom rules (mercy and grace
freely extended to all)? The daily seeds of submission we plant
both knowingly and unknowingly will have lifelong consequences for our children. For good or for ill, our kids usually
end up doing what we do and not what we say.

Let's say there is a situation in which you often react in

anger. Perhaps it's when you are kept waiting in a doctor's office despite having a scheduled appointment now long past. The first time you envision this imaginary-but-real scene, allow yourself to react "badly." Get the frustration out of your system. Then go through it again, and this time behave graciously. You do not have to deny the injustice, wrongness, or difficulty of the situation. The Discipline of Submission does not ask us to lie to ourselves about the realities of hard circumstances or other people's tricky temperaments; it simply asks us to try as much as we can to respond to those situations or people as Jesus would.

Repeat this exercise until you begin to alter your public behavior on a regular basis.

5. Learn as much as you can about the practice of consensus, and then act upon what you learn. Consensus is one of the absolutely joyous ways we have seen submission to others work really well. Reaching consensus as a body, or family, of people can come only when we intentionally listen to others. When a meeting is run by consensus—whether in business or in the home—people are required to listen to what everyone else has to say. It does not take courage to speak up, as it often does in authoritarian or majority-rule circumstances when your lifted voice can be drowned in the din of people stomping on your sense of self. Instead, consensus requires sublimating our own will and deferring resolutions and actions until others have had an opportunity to weigh in on whatever matter is before us.

Cutting short or railroading people is not allowed. Everyone is permitted a full voice. Reaching consensus requires respect for another's viewpoint; consensus can never be reached if we do not mutually submit to each other and acknowledge the legitimacy of someone else's perspective. Some family decisions can be reached through consensus (such as which video to watch), and others cannot (such as how much to spend on groceries in a given week).

Of course, this is not a quick way to do business. Decisions may need postponement until all can come to a place of accord. However, when individuals submit to one another in order to reach consensus, they invite God into the decision-making process and are much more likely to see him at work in people's lives. Most of us have much to learn from our Quaker brothers and sisters who, as a basic tenet of their faith, always seek to build consensus before taking action.

TEACHING THE DISCIPLINE

In teaching the Discipline of Submission to our children, our aim is to help them understand that they are not the center of the universe—God is. And anytime we allow children to have yet another experience of pouting their way into a position of power, we are enabling them to believe that the world revolves around them rather than around their Creator.

As you seek to teach this discipline to your children, use wisdom and discernment. The needs and desires of our little ones are not inevitably subordinate to ours. At times, parents need to submit to children and give them the time and attention they need now, at the present moment. If our children are feeling emotionally overwrought—perhaps a bully stole their lunch money or another child said something mean on the playground—we need to listen right then and there. We need to comfort emotional wounds in the same way we attend to physical ones. We don't want to encourage submission to bullies or mean-spirited classmates.

Another caution: We both know—probably you do too—people who have abused the Discipline of Submission under the guise of "obeying God's law" and "training children up for the Lord." Any kind of parental discipline that brings a thrill of authority and power is wrong. Submission must be extracted with humility and the goal of raising children who have strong self-esteem, know they are loved, and in that love, are held accountable for their actions. Whatever else you may remember about this discipline, please keep in mind at all times that it is one of love, not clout.

EARLY CHILDHOOD (*ages 4–7*):

1. When friends are coming over to play, ask your children if there is anything that they don't want to share. Put it away where it won't be a source of contention. At this age, children are learning to be hospitable, but feeling proprietary about certain toys is a developmental stage that not all youngsters are ready to get past just yet. However, don't allow your children to put away more than one toy before visitors arrive.

2. Help your kids begin to understand the rules of hospitality. Remind them that they never need to have those friends over again to play, but that during the event, they must show kindness toward their guests. If it turns out to be a difficult situation,

intervene as the adult and set some boundaries on the other children's behavior. That way, you can teach that although we should always begin relationships in good faith, when a line gets crossed, we are allowed to stand up for ourselves.

3. Never cave in to your children's whining and pleading. This teaches them to continue that kind of behavior until they get what they want from their parents, their teachers, and later on, their spouses and children. If you are used to giving in to temper tantrums, it will take some time to break the habit. Leave the store as soon as a temper tantrum begins, even if it means the errands you came to do go unfinished. If your children whine or get angry at home, insist on a time-out alone in their rooms until they can talk calmly about what it is they feel they need.

4. Don't make your children always wait around for you to play with them or help them with a project. But do teach them that when you are on the phone or talking to someone else, they are not to interrupt except in the case of an emergency.

5. Insist that kids come quickly when called with no yelling back or procrastinating allowed. They need to learn to respond instantly to our voices because sometimes there is imminent danger they may not see or understand.

MIDDLE CHILDHOOD (ages 8–11):

1. Keep the ideas going that are mentioned in the "Early Childhood" section.

2. Help your kids start a "frustration journal." Get an inexpensive notebook and allow them to write anything they want in the

notebook. When your children are upset or angry, bring out their journals and encourage them to write hard and furiously. After the initial feelings are out on paper, offer to listen to what they want to share about the situation.

Remind them that it would not be appropriate to say heated things to the person who caused the anger, that deliberately hurting someone else in defense of "honesty" is wrong. However, the angry feeling itself is not wrong; it is only when we act on that feeling to get back at someone else that our behavior becomes inappropriate. Hold regular consecration sessions in which the journal and its writings are committed to God for safekeeping. The pages ready for consecration might be burned or shredded. They might even stay in the journal with a penned message of a different color slanting crosswise across the page that reads, "In God's Hands."

3. Do not allow your kids to bully younger siblings. Immediately shut down bribery, name-calling, shoving, and rude language as it relates to siblings, classmates, and friends.

4. If you have only two children, consider using the odd/even system for privileges and responsibilities. Identify which child is "odd" and which is "even." Use the calendar's odd and even days as the key to settling disputes. If there is an argument, for example, about who gets to choose the TV station or who has to brush the cat, the calendar date resolves the quarrel. Because seven of the months have thirty-one days, making two odd days in a row, flip a coin on that last day of the month should a dispute come up. Valerie used this system with her children

and they appreciated the fairness of it even if they didn't immediately like the result. Yours will too.

ADOLESCENCE (ages 12–15):

1. Journaling is a good skill for young people to develop, if they
   haven't already. Adolescents suffer more than their share of
   angst brought about by physical maturation, unfamiliar hor-
   mones, and peer group norms. Encourage them to write down
   their feelings as a way of talking with God about them. But,
   above all, be sure to respect the privacy of those writings and
   absolutely *never* look at them uninvited.
2. Do your best to help your teens feel good about themselves.
   Kids who have a solid sense of self don't need to always have
   their own way. Find ways to affirm your child in this very difficult transitional time period.
3. Choose your battles carefully. Teens are going through a natural
   phase of individuating their personalities from ours. They will
   not submit as easily to our will as they did when they were
   younger, and this is to be expected. In truth, what we want
   them to avoid are unsafe activities, such as drugs and alcohol,
   premarital sex, and reckless driving. As they experiment with
   growing independence, let some of the clothing and hair battles
   go, and focus on their behaviors and attitudes instead, especially those that could lead to harmful habits. Respect them as
   individuals, allow them the room to grow and discover who
   they are, but don't let them get away with temper tantrums,
   screaming matches, and rude behavior. By keeping a firm stand

on important issues and letting nonessential issues go (hair grows out, clothing styles inevitably change), you are more likely to be listened to.

4. Help your adolescents find a volunteer position that allows them to see how hierarchies work. If it is at an organization that is trying to address some injustice in society, your teens can begin to gain some insight about how one handles or doesn't handle injustices in the larger society.

THE BOTTOM LINE

While the Discipline of Submission has cautions attached to it, because of its liberating aspects and attention to the needs of others, it is one of the most important disciplines for grounding ourselves in God and in relationship to family, friends, and neighbors. It is a discipline that is not gender-specific or age-specific; we are to mutually submit to each other. Through mutual submission, we are freed to be who we are meant to be and not who position demands we be.

Chapter Eight

THE DISCIPLINE OF SERVICE

The evening meal was being served. . . . Jesus knew that the Father
had put all things under his power, and that he had come from God
and was returning to God; so he got up from the meal, took off
his outer clothing, and wrapped a towel around his waist. After that,
he poured water into a basin and began to wash his disciples' feet,
drying them with the towel that was wrapped around him.

Jᴏʜɴ 13:2-5

Uɴᴅᴇʀsᴛᴀɴᴅɪɴɢ ᴛʜᴇ Dɪsᴄɪᴘʟɪɴᴇ

Fred Garlett, Marti's husband, has the heart of a servant. Nothing
is too big or small for him to take on if it benefits someone else.
He feeds cats, walks dogs, gathers newspapers, mows lawns, cleans
gutters, buys groceries, paints walls, builds fences, prepares simple
meals, does laundry, takes cars in for tune-ups, and does practically
anything else that he sees a family member or neighbor needs help
with. He even runs his office as a servant leader. His philosophy, as
"the boss," is that he is there to support others, not the other way
around. Fred views his role as a simple one: He is there to ensure
the success of those who work for him.

Interestingly enough, for years while he was growing up, Fred's
family took over the care and feeding of an infirm elderly couple living nearby. The physical work of mowing and painting was left to
Fred and his brother, while his mother and sister handled grocery

shopping and food preparation. By the time Fred left home, service had become an ingrained holy habit.

When we train ourselves—and our children—in the Discipline of Service, it can become our habit as well.

The Plumb Line of Service

Our goal in the Discipline of Service is an attitude of servanthood, a way of thinking that has outward manifestations. Our motivation for serving others comes solely out of our love for God and others and our desire to be like Jesus.

To better train ourselves in becoming true servants, we need to understand the differences between true service and self-righteous service. In contrast to true service, self-righteous service, says Richard Foster, requires external rewards: "It needs to know that people see and appreciate the effort. It seeks human applause—with proper religious modesty of course. True service rests contented in hiddenness. It does not fear the lights and blare of attention, but it does not seek them either."[1]

In addition, Foster points out that:

- Self-righteous service prefers to do deeds of titanic proportions. True service finds it almost impossible to distinguish the small from the large.
- Self-righteous service calculates results and expects reciprocity. True service delights only in the service itself.
- Self-righteous service picks and chooses whom to serve, mostly because of gaining a coveted public image. True

service is indiscriminate in its ministry and almost never notices whether others are watching.

- Moods and whims affect self-righteous service. True service ministers simply and faithfully because there is a need.
- Self-righteous service is temporary. Having served, it rests easy. True service is an ongoing lifestyle.
- Self-righteous service puts others into the servant's debt. True service quietly and unpretentiously goes about caring for others' needs, putting no one under obligation to return the service.[2]

True service springs from a heart of compassion and humility, a heart like Jesus'. Jesus did not direct his compassion only to individuals caught up in tragic circumstances beyond their control. If we are seeking to be his disciples, we will be open to serving anyone who has a need—even those we think have created their own personal crises.

_____

How can I possibly serve others in unfeigned humility if I seriously regard their sinfulness as worse than my own?

DIETRICH BONHOEFFER

_____

Keeping Service in Balance

In practicing this discipline, we must understand that we are not infinite. We only have a limited amount of time, energy, and resources. Only God can "cover the waterfront."

Like all the disciplines, we need to keep this one in balance. Sometimes the good turns we do for others become our most important priority. In other words, we can spend so much time volunteering and helping at church, ministries, or humanitarian agencies that we have no time left for personal restoration, worship, or our families. When service is out of balance, it moves us away from, rather than toward, God. It drains rather than restores.

St. Theresa said that to give our Lord a perfect service, Martha and Mary must combine. . . . Thousands of devoted men and women today believe that the really good part is to keep busy, and give themselves no time to take what is offered to those who abide quietly with Christ, because there seem such a lot of urgent jobs for Martha to do. The result of this can only be a maiming of their human nature, exhaustion, loss of depth and of vision, and it is seen in the vagueness and ineffectuality of a great deal of the work that is done for God.

EVELYN UNDERHILL

We see this principle in the story of Mary and Martha (see Luke 10:38-42; John 11:1-44; John 12:1-11). Remember what happened? Jesus went to Mary and Martha's for dinner. Mary wanted to be with him and sat at his feet, worshiping, while her sister Martha was hard at work in the kitchen, serving. Martha got in a snit because Mary wasn't helping her, and so Martha complained to Jesus about it. In response, he said,

"Mary has chosen the better part" (Luke 10:42, NRSV).

When we put this story in the context of all of Scripture, it's clear that God values both worship and service and that we are not to engage in one at the expense of the other. In her excellent book *Having a Mary Heart in a Martha World*, Joanna Weaver writes:

> How do we choose the Better Part and still get done what really has to be done?
>
> Jesus is our supreme example. He was never in a hurry. He knew who he was and where he was going. He wasn't held hostage to the world's demands or even its desperate needs. "I only do what the Father tells me to do," Jesus told his disciples.[3]

When we practice the other disciplines, particularly the Discipline of Worship, we are more likely to keep service in its proper place and know what acts of service God would have us do. Worship keeps our hearts humble and reminds us that God loves us because he is love and because of who we are in Jesus Christ, not because of all the good things we do.

Service Should Bring Us Joy

It helps us keep service in balance when we look for *regular* service opportunities that fit with our gifts. This is important, as we will see needs everywhere, and if we don't have some sense of where we can best serve, we are apt to do more harm than good.

This was brought home to me (Valerie) several years ago. After church one Sunday, a deacon asked me to help an elderly woman use the restroom. Obviously, he could not help, and I felt caught, not knowing how to say "no." It was an awful experience. The older woman was embarrassed, and I nearly got sick. It would have been much better if I would have said, "Let me find someone who is more qualified to help her." I now remind myself regularly that God has spread gifts throughout the body of Christ and that the things that cause me dread and drudgery will bring another person joy and delight.

Joy, not grit, is the hallmark of holy obedience.

RICHARD FOSTER

Of course, even within our calling and gifts, we will always have to do some tasks that will not thrill and inspire us. Not every moment of service will be a mountaintop experience. Drudgery will always be with us. Someone has to take out the garbage and clean the toilets, and even if we love baking for others, somebody has to do the dishes.

But here is the tension: We don't get extra points by being miserable week after week at the homeless shelter or soup kitchen if street people frighten or anger us. We are not extra godly working in our child's classroom if groups of kids give us headaches. Exhaustion will not win us extra merit badges with God. To guard against this, we can ask God and our faith community to help us discern an area of service that will bring us joy. Where God has gifted us, there is a niche for us to fill. Let's be faithful in looking for it.

*The place where God calls you to is the place where
your deep gladness and the world's deep hunger meet.*

FREDERICK BUECHNER

The Discipline of Service begins with humility and ends with humility. Christian humility is not walking around with a sign on our forehead that says, "Run over me, please." Just as Jesus, the Creator and Lord of all, humbled himself and washed the feet of his disciples—even the one who was going to betray him—we can humbly serve others because we know who we are: children of God. This knowing frees us to have the heart of a servant, even if we can't fulfill the need in front of us at the moment.

*Lord, let me make a difference for you that is utterly
disproportionate to who I am.*

JOHN PIPER

PRACTICING THE DISCIPLINE

The goal in this discipline is to pinpoint those times in which we are serving for the wrong reasons or in a wrong spirit. Use the following suggestions to help you look at your attitudes and gifts:

1. So much of this discipline comes from the inside out. Begin by tracking your service attitude for a week. Every time you're asked to do something for someone else, note how you feel. Jot

it down in a notebook to assess at the end of the week. How many times did you feel "put out" or like a martyr? How many times did you feel you were working out of your gifts? Did you feel angry because nobody commented on how hard you worked, how well you did, and so on? Ask your spouse or a close friend if he or she sees you with a servant's heart. Accept the answer in humility and use it to begin praying for more of the spirit of service that was in Jesus.

2. Find a project for which you receive no personal benefit. Take a trash bag to the park and pick up litter. Shovel the neighbor's driveway anonymously. Offer to walk a neighbor's dog regularly and pick up after it. Leave a public restroom cleaner than when you found it.

3. Look for a regular act of service in your area of giftedness. First, ask yourself what kinds of things you like to do. What tasks, activities, or responsibilities bring you joy and gladness? Where might you be able to meet a need with those skills? Then, begin to pray and to seek counsel from others about how that joy and delight might be used to serve others. Never discount something you like to do as being too small to be of service to someone.

4. Find a way to get out of volunteer jobs that cause you to grit your teeth. (See pages 89–90 for tips on saying "no" to people and situations.) Ask God to show you places where you can use your gifts and talents in joy. For example, if you said "yes" to being membership chair for the PTA, but organizational skills are not your gift, admit your mistake and work to find someone who is good at organizing and administrating. If cooking is your forte,

volunteer to provide a certain amount of food for school events.

5. Look for ways to express gratitude in each necessary task you do, particularly those you dislike or view as drudgery. Every situation has something to be thankful for, even if it is limited to God's promised presence in it with us. My husband, John, does this well. For instance, when he pays our bills each month, he thanks God for how richly we've been provided for. His attitude of thanksgiving in all circumstances demonstrates that even though we may not always have a choice about what we have to do, we always have a choice over our attitude.

TEACHING THE DISCIPLINE

The Disciplines of Service and Submission are close cousins. We can help our kids learn humility and service by insisting they help with household chores and show respect toward others. Serving others should be as much a part of our children's lives as school is.

Here are some overarching principles before we list age-specific ideas:

1. Nurture an attitude of service in everyone. For instance, don't let older children tyrannize younger ones. Encourage your kids to help you, each other, and people with obvious needs, such as those with disabilities.
2. Don't allow your kids to speak negatively about others or to be rude or loudmouthed, even if they are right. Teach them to express frustration and anger in ways that focus on the issue, not the person.

3. Help kids learn how to receive kindness graciously. Teach them not to belittle other people's high regard of them. If someone compliments them, teach them to say thank you and enjoy the praise. Kids with good self-esteem won't become braggarts. They will have a solid sense of self and be able to relish their own achievements as well as the achievements of others. Being a good receiver is part of being a good server.

4. We also can teach children, no matter their age, that prayer is a form of service. Encourage your kids to serve by praying for the world's problems. For example if they see pictures of starving children, pray with them, asking God to provide resources for those children. Better yet, "adopt" a child through an aid organization that sends regular help to kids with few resources. The pictures and periodic letters that come from those children will touch your family. Praying and caring for one person in need out of the billions in the world who are needy is a manageable task.

5. Guide your kids toward a passion to learn skills that will be useful to them and society as a whole. Start by reading books about occupations to your younger children. Listen with respect to their ideas of what they want to be when they grow up. Be encouraging of their dreams when they are little. Even though those goals may change many times over the years, the freedom to dream can help them identify their areas of giftedness. However, be wary of telling your older children that they can do anything they want, as this may overwhelm them. By the time they are in high school, you can begin to help them discern their unique gifts.

EARLY CHILDHOOD (*ages 4–7*):

1. Don't allow young children to act up during meals and phone calls because "they are too little to understand." Kids need to learn from age three on that there are times when their demands are not top priority.

2. If you have yard space or a patio for some container gardening, have your kids help you plant and care for some flowers. Together, make a bouquet out of the flowers and give them to someone who needs cheering up. Talk with your kids about why you are doing this.

3. Even young children can participate in household chores: putting their toys away when finished playing, clearing their dishes from the table after a meal, helping you make their bed and pick up their room, helping feed the family pets, hanging their towels up after their baths, putting their dirty clothes in the hamper, and replacing the toothpaste cap on the tube after brushing their teeth.

4. Take your young children to the grocery store to buy supplies for a shut-in, and then deliver the groceries together. If possible, allow your kids to pick out some flowers or a special treat from the bakery to add to the necessities. An added bonus is that someone who gets out very little or not at all will enjoy briefly chatting with a young child, thereby teaching that spending time with someone is an important form of service.

MIDDLE CHILDHOOD (*ages 8–11*):

1. Instead of letting your kids come up with excuses for not participating in acts of service, guide them toward service activities in which they can use their gifts and talents. For example, if your son is in a scout troop and the scouts are going to do a service project, insist that he participate as part of his membership in the group. However, if he never enjoys any of the troop's service projects, talk with him about whether he should be involved in another activity better suited to his personality, interests, and abilities.

2. Together, read a biography of someone who overcame difficult circumstances, such as Abraham Lincoln, Martin Luther King, or Clara Barton. Ask your librarian for more suggestions. As you read, talk about what was hard in the person's background. Discuss some of the ways that individual worked to overcome those deficiencies. Talk about how the hardships that person faced growing up helped him or her to serve others later.

3. Start a "secret buddy" program. Discuss with your children someone they know who may be in need. Plan a way for your children to secretly reach out to that person. For example, if there is an elderly person living alone in your neighborhood, have your children make a card to put on that person's door.

4. Do not pay your children for doing chores. It can cause them to feel that service is conditional on rewards for self. Help them see that they are part of a family and that everyone pitches in for the good of the group.

ADOLESCENCE *(ages 12–15):*

1. Plan a field trip or vacation to help those less fortunate than you. One family we know (husband, wife, children, their spouses, and a couple of grandchildren) transported toys and clothes on a self-funded Christmas vacation to Guatemala to deliver gifts to children living in poverty. This was the family's present to each other; no other gifts were exchanged that year, though each individual's Spanish-speaking skills were definitely honed, a marvelous gift in itself.

2. Help your kids begin the lifelong habit of tithing by encouraging teens to give 10 percent of their money to your church and charitable institutions. (Decide as a family if gift money needs to be tithed. The Hess family tithes only money earned by working.)

3. Encourage your young teens to find a volunteer job. Not only does this help when they begin applying to college, but it also teaches some important spiritual lessons: We don't need to get paid for everything we do, and our worth to others is not measured by dollars and cents. This helps teach our children to operate on a different economic system than that of our culture.

THE BOTTOM LINE

The Discipline of Service means that we develop the attitude of Christ toward others, working to weed out the self-righteous attitudes. It means we understand our gifts and talents and seek to use those in regular ways to help the world around us.

Chapter Nine

THE DISCIPLINE OF CONFESSION

Therefore confess your sins to each other and pray for each other so that you may be healed. The prayer of a righteous [person] is powerful and effective.

JAMES 5:16

UNDERSTANDING THE DISCIPLINE

The Discipline of Confession allows us to enter the grace and mercy of God in such a way that we experience healing of our past sins and forgive those who have sinned against us. Without a doubt, parents must represent the face of God to their children under this discipline. My (Marti's) mother helped me understand the value of confession very early in life by providing me with a godly example.

When I was about four or five years old, I shoplifted a tiny pack of animal rummy cards from a dime store. I hid them in my jacket pocket and, when I got home, played with them all afternoon in the bathroom, the only room whose door locked. Obviously, I knew I had done something wrong. Before the afternoon was over, my mother discovered my theft. Even though the town with the dime store was far away and dinnertime was drawing near, my mother piled me into our old black Buick with the running board and took me back to the scene of the crime. While my mother stood immovably near, I confessed my sin to the store manager and apologized, handing over the stolen items.

I can still remember the tears of hot shame and the painful burning in my cheeks. My mother then marched me back to the car, took me in her arms, and told me she loved me and was proud of me for having made a wrong right. Out-of-control four-year-olds can grow up to be out-of-control fourteen-year-olds unless a parent takes decisive steps. I thank God my mother did.

A child of the light confesses instantly and stands bared
before God; a child of the darkness says,
"Oh, I can explain that away."

OSWALD CHAMBERS

The Two Go Hand in Hand

Confession would have done me no good as a little girl if I had been allowed to keep the cards and continue playing with them. No, confession works only when we take explicit, concrete steps that walk us away from committing the same offense again. The humiliation of handing back stolen goods was a memorable step in that direction for me. Repentance (confession) and redemption (forgiveness coupled with Jesus' commandment to go and sin no more) work together to enable healing. Without repentance, we will not experience redemption. And without redemption, confession rings hollow and consists of empty words spoken into a vacuum.

Parents can model repentance by apologizing when they use insensitive language or when they ignore or abruptly dismiss their children's honest questions. Because we parents are human, we can find many opportunities to demonstrate confession to our kids. And we can show redemption by forgiving their wrongdoings and presenting the human face of Christ to them in our own countenance.

We both know young people who have been fortunate enough to have the kind of parents to whom it is safe to confess any number of truly terrible transgressions. Sexually active girls who become pregnant and seek abortions or boys who have taken drugs and become addicts are some sad and serious examples that come to mind. In order for these children to get their lives back on a godly track, they need parents who understand the twin forces of repentance and redemption and can represent Christ in their troubled teens' lives. There is nothing easy about this, of course. We work hard to master the spiritual disciplines so that at extremely difficult times we have God's own resources to call upon.

Our great redemption from above did bring;
For so the holy sages once did sing,
That He our deadly forfeit should release,
And with His Father work us a perpetual peace.

JOHN MILTON

Public Confession Is Essential

Oswald Chambers writes in his classic devotional *My Utmost for His Highest* that "sin must die out in me, not be curbed or suppressed or counteracted, but crucified."[1]

Crucifixions such as the one Jesus endured were carried out on very public stages. And so it must be with confession. But the idea of public confession can be terrifying. It's one thing to confess your sins to God in private; it's quite another to confess them to others, no matter how warm or kindhearted the people might be. Our pride that someone else will fully see us as we are—broken and imperfect—sometimes keeps us from seeking the spiritual help we need. The act of confession forces us to lay down our pride and humbly admit to our shortcomings and sins. It's impossible to make a confession with a proud heart, and so we must, for the sake of our own healthy souls, undergo the humility of doing it in public.

For years, a father, whom I'll call David, was fearful of apologizing to his children, expecting that all his authority would be lost if he did. He recognized when he made mistakes or spoke too harshly or was benignly neglectful, but he would not admit these parental failings to anyone other than himself.

Finally, he brought a tale of remorse to his wife. "There was no need for me to yell at Jamie when he drank right from the mouth of the milk carton," he confessed to her. "I wish I had handled that with more gentleness. I wish I could do it all over."

"Why can't you?" she asked, which made him stop and think about the deeper meaning her words conveyed.

And so he sought out his twelve-year-old son and apologized to him. David did not retract the point he was trying to make—that everyone in the family drinks milk from the same carton and that if certain food standards aren't maintained, lack of proper sanitation poses a possible health risk to others. But he did apologize for the words he had chosen, the tone he had used, and the way he had handled the situation. His son's quick forgiveness and ready warmth surprised David. The fact is, his son had seen him—maybe for the first time—as a human being worthy of intimate relationship.

Confession of our faults is the next thing to innocence.

PUBLILIUS SYRUS

God Is Infinitely Merciful

Just as David's son showed mercy to his father, so the Discipline of Confession reveals the infinite mercy of God. Though we ask how it can be—because it is not like this in our human world where the "three strikes" rule reigns—God's mercy never exhausts itself. It can and does go on and on, exponentially greater in number and larger in scope than any sins we will ever commit. This is tremendously good news. We and our children should receive and learn to rely upon this gift of mercy during the daily course of our lives. God's grace is available to all who ask, but the "asking" must come through the act of confession, which is why grace is so inextricably entwined with public declaration of guilt.

We are forgiven long before we repent. Experiencing that forgiveness, however, requires that we repent.

JIM SMITH

PRACTICING THE DISCIPLINE

Confession is not at all easy when we first begin to practice it. We live in a world filled with artifice where, in the words of the comic, "it's better to look good than feel good." We don't want people seeing behind our chosen façades. We are ashamed to admit our faults. We want to keep firmly intact the public face we prefer, the one that suggests ever-present steadiness and stability and everything being forever right with our world. Despite my mother's early teaching, I confess that this is still a very difficult discipline for me. It makes me uncomfortable, sometimes desperately so, and yet I know from experience that it is one of the most important God-given devices for releasing me from the bondage of sin and keeping me directly linked to my Savior.

1. If you worship in a liturgical church where confession to the priest or pastor is common, use this availability joyfully and frequently. Use it in the same way you make appointments for medical and dental checkups. Even though we don't look forward to being poked and prodded by a doctor, such checkups are critical. They save our health and sometimes our lives. In a spiritual sense, confession saves our souls.

    If your church does not overtly practice this discipline—or if you have never confessed your sins to others—we want to encourage you to push through your resistance or awkwardness with the idea. Begin by asking a mature Christian friend to meet with you regularly for the purpose of confession and accountability. Another way to think about it is to ask yourself this question: *Who around you, even if only an acquaintance, might desire the same kind of growth in faith you are seeking?* Maybe it is your spouse. Whoever it is, approach this person prayerfully about the idea.

If he or she says "yes," start with small struggles as you begin to get to know each other. Test the waters little by little. As your partner proves to be faithful and able to keep confidences, your trust will grow to take on larger issues. And when a friend is engaged with you in the process, both of you grow closer to each other and to God. Through mutual confession, you will have shared the same ground at the foot of the Cross.

If you remain unsure about whom to ask, pray that God would reveal a person you should approach or that he would bring such a person into your life. Then keep your eyes open at church, work, Bible study, or any situation in which you regularly interact with others. But if a sin is weighing you down, don't wait until you have located a partner; go to clergy or another Christian professional counselor and confess that sin. Sometimes unconfessed sin weighs a person down so heavily, deep depression sets in and—let's say it aloud—suicide can result. Unconfessed sin is not something to be taken lightly. It can be deadly.

Both of us have been members of a Renovaré group. (Renovaré is the small-group movement that grew out of Richard Foster's book *Celebration of Discipline*.) We found it a safe harbor where we could hold ourselves accountable to other adults for practicing all twelve of the spiritual disciplines, including the Discipline of Confession.

2. The Discipline of Confession must become part of your home's
internal weather. As with all the disciplines, modeling is critical when it comes to teaching it. Let your children know that
you practice this discipline, and discuss with them why you
do. Even more important, be willing to acknowledge any
wrongdoings you have done to them, such as when you have
been impatient or harsh with them. Tell them specifically why
you are sorry and ask their forgiveness. That doesn't mean you
need to change a decision, such as having said "no" to a child's
request. It only means your apology should come from the type
of communication you may have used to convey that "no"—
that is, your tone and words.

Don't be afraid to express genuine regrets for your behavior
to your kids. They need to hear this from you so that they can
emulate it. They need to know it is okay to feel remorseful about
something that has happened in the family and to say so. Initiate
concrete steps to make restitution, and then avoid making the
same mistake again. For example, one parent I know became so
irritated at her daughter that she threw her little girl's doll at the
wall, smashing its head. Not only was an act of contrition in
order, so was restitution through replacement of the toy.

TEACHING THE DISCIPLINE

Children often feel powerless to change their behavior. Nevertheless,
they can find healing and freedom through the Discipline of
Confession by admitting they were wrong, resolving to do right, and,

with help, mapping out a specific course of action that will lead them away from repeating the same troubling behavior.

EARLY CHILDHOOD (ages 4–7):

1. When young children have done something wrong, help them understand the broader consequences. Talk with them specifically about how others were affected by their actions and words. Go with them to make the apology and, if necessary, arrange for restitution. This method of teaching the Discipline of Confession spans all age levels and demonstrates the redemptive value of public confession.

2. Apologize to your kids immediately whenever you lose your temper with them. The way in which you communicate must be both loving and appropriate, even if the issue that caused your initial anger remains unchanged. Don't mumble your apology, and be sure (especially for this age group) to hold them tight as you offer your sorrow to them.

3. Children this age love to role-play. They love to dress up and move themselves into a land of characters whose script is spontaneously written by them. Little girls may "build" schoolrooms for their stuffed toys and act as the teacher, sternly telling the inanimate creatures how to behave. Little boys, even if deliberately not provided with toy guns, will almost certainly make them of their own fingers. They are in charge of their universe when they're caught up in "power play."

   We can invite ourselves to enter this pretend territory with them. We too can assume a costume of some sort (even if it is nothing but a hat), change our voices, and create imaginary scenes with words that are crafted in the moment. Our children not only welcome us when we do this, they are delighted. At such times, we can set up a scenario in which an act of contrition is required. No one, of course, will really get hurt. The purpose is to help teach during play that people can do wrong things, inadvertently or deliberately, but that forgiveness and reconciliation can take place too.

Here's a simple "for instance." During a tea party with his five-year-old daughter, Daddy holds a tiny tea cup in his big hand and "accidentally" drops it. He immediately offers an apology for his clumsiness and asks his daughter if he can have another cup, with which he promises to be more careful. Later, when the party is over, he can talk in more depth about how important it is to say we're sorry when we do something that disturbs someone else, even when our deeds are unintentional.

Middle Childhood (*ages 8–11*):

1. This is probably more of a caveat to keep in mind than an actual teaching idea, but it nevertheless is so important that we want to include it here. When a playmate has sinned against one of your children, it can take time for trust to be restored. Perhaps a teammate snatched your son's favorite baseball cap on the school bus and threw it out the window. Perhaps a close friend's gossip harmed your daughter's reputation. Your child will need time to get over the hurt. Even if the person who committed the offense apologizes to your child, it may take

some time for him or her to want to play with or be around
that person again. Children are not only injured by the act
committed against them, they are equally hurt and confused by
truly awful conduct from any trusted friend. Deep wounding
may occur in a friendship, even when an apology is offered. If
the friend never apologizes, be prepared to explain that not
everyone apologizes when he or she should.

Don't rush the process. When feelings have been torn asun-
der, refrain from insisting that everything go back to normal.
Forgiveness does not necessarily need to mean business as
usual. Both of us have come to forgive people for deep hurts,
though neither of us spend much time with those individuals
anymore. You can probably think of an incident or two in your
own life in which this is true as well.

2. Insist on your children owning up to their actions and words
   despite extenuating circumstances. An all too fallible human
   reaction to deliberately seek vengeance against those who have
   wronged us begins to rear its ugly head around this age. Don't
   let your kids use other people or the event itself to justify
   wrong choices. Help them see that in all circumstances, they
   have options about how they will respond and that they, and
   no one else, bear responsibility for which option they choose.
   Settling of scores or retaliation never can be justified.

   Sometimes sporting events, if your children are participating in them, can serve as the perfect context for this type of
   conversation. For example, someone fouls your child and gets
   away with it; the referee doesn't see it happen. Your angry child

wants to retaliate. It is this lashing out, eye-for-an-eye impulse you want to help your children learn to control. Teach that, in Christ, the seventy-seven-times forgiveness rule reigns (see Matthew 18:21-22).

3. Watch the evening news or, better yet, read a daily newspaper with your children. Locate local or world events in which forgiveness is required. The news is rife with such occurrences. Discuss which parties involved in the incident need to make a confession and to whom they should make it. How difficult will forgiveness be in this case? What individual or group will need to grant the forgiveness? Through what processes could redemption for the sinner and then reconciliation with the injured parties occur? How might the first step be taken?

ADOLESCENCE *(ages 12–15):*

1. It is especially important for young teenagers to learn they are responsible for their own actions, if for no other reason than that in the eyes of the law they are held culpable for what they do, regardless of what their friends did or did not do.

   For example, most adolescents, as soon as they hit their teen years, look forward to getting their driver's license. Driving a vehicle holds them legally responsible for their own actions as well as those of their passengers. Everything from passengers not wearing seatbelts to carrying open containers of alcohol carries liability for the driver. If passengers pressure the driver to run a red light and the driver does so, blame for an accident or the cost of the ticket sits squarely in the driver's lap

and no one else's. The tag of "guilty" goes to only one person—the driver. Start having these sorts of conversations with
your adolescent youngsters *now*.

2. Help young teens find appropriate ways to express frustrations
   before they turn their internalized feelings into inappropriate
   actions. Journaling can be a good tool. Encourage them to
   write honestly how they really feel about a person or situation.
   This kind of journal can include pictures. Help your kids
   assess what they can do to change a situation, but, again, *never*
   read their journals without explicit invitation.

Instead of additional ideas, we want to offer an important stip-
ulation here: We must *listen* to our adolescent youngsters before
we jump to conclusions about their behavior. They are more likely
to be less communicative with us at this time of their lives than at
any other. Remember, they're in a transition; they will and must
assert their independence from us. If, for example, they are told to
come straight home after school but do not, we first need to listen
to their reasons before assigning blame or expecting them to own
up to a mistake. Sometimes there really are extenuating circumstances that are quite understandable.

When I was dating my husband, we were in the backseat of a
car driven by another boy who had his girlfriend with him. He
drove straight to a park for what we called in those days "parking."
Fred did not take advantage of this situation. Instead, he walked
me home and then walked to his own home a couple of miles away.
We were older than young adolescents, to be sure, but even so, we

both could have been in trouble for arriving home quite a bit later than expected (there were no cell phones in the 1960s). Thankfully, our parents listened to us before arriving at any conclusions. And because they did, we were pardoned.

THE BOTTOM LINE

The Discipline of Confession allows us to enter the grace and mercy of God in such a way that we experience the healing of all past sins. The glorious by-product of this discipline is a therapeutic one. Through verbal profession of our wrongdoings, we are released from the crushing oppression of our own sins or the sins of those who committed duplicitous acts against us. Liberation through grace is the gift that forgiveness of self and others conveys to us.

Chapter Ten

THE DISCIPLINE OF WORSHIP

Worship the LORD with gladness;
come before him with joyful songs.

———————

PSALM 100:2

UNDERSTANDING THE DISCIPLINE

The Discipline of Worship helps us develop a life dedicated to giving God honor and glory in all that we say and do. It reminds us that *we* are not the center of the universe—*God* is, and therefore he is worthy of our worship. Oswald Chambers says that in worship we are to "[give] God the best that he has given [us]."[1] We are invited—even called—to give God center place in our family relationships, work, recreation, money, and bodies.

I (Valerie) learned some valuable lessons about worship when my husband and I moved to St. Louis for graduate school and attended a Presbyterian church that was in a racially mixed neighborhood. One of the unusual characteristics of this church was the way worship was understood and practiced. Anyone joining this church committed to three things: coming regularly to a particular service (as each service had its own time and focus), coming to congregational meetings (out of 200 members, 198 would be at the meeting), and being a faithful member of a midweek prayer group.

Our family committed to the service that met at four o'clock on Sunday afternoons. After church ended at 5:30, we would all eat a potluck meal together. It was organized so that our menus, seating assignments, and even the tasks of setting up and cleaning up rotated from week to week. Our prayer group met Wednesday nights for worship and prayer, and occasionally we did fun activities as a group outside the Wednesday night time frame.

While everything centered on our worship times on Sundays, the results of our corporate worship life spilled over visibly into our lives the rest of the week. We reached out to our church neighbors through various ministries the church oversaw: affordable housing for low-income residents, a food co-op, outreach programs for the kids, and so on. Our weekly prayer group meetings fed back into the corporate worship time, which strengthened our ties with our community.

That community taught me many graphic lessons about worship, including this one: As Christians, we are called to live a "seamless life."

A Seamless Life

A seamless life is a life that makes no distinction between sacred things and secular things. In other words, sitting at a sporting event and cheering our favorite team can be as much an act of worship as sitting in a pew on Sunday morning. If the definition of worship is giving honor and glory to God, then we can be worshiping God at a ball game as well as in a church service. When we live a seamless life, the language we use, the way we treat those around us, and our attitude will all be the same from one venue to the next.

This way of looking at life as constant worship elevates some tasks (changing diapers, washing dishes, mowing the grass) and keeps other tasks (teaching Sunday school, volunteering at the hospital, being a pastor) off false pedestals. Meaning, if we are the same person cleaning up the kitchen as we are preaching or teaching, then we are giving honor and glory to God in everything we do. Notice how this attitude overlaps with the crux of the Discipline of Service. We simply live for God's honor and glory in all that we say and do (or don't say and don't do). Therefore, we can worship God whether we are doing it in a corporate setting, in our Bible reading time at home, or while going about the required tasks of the day.

Corporate Versus Private Worship

When we have a seamless view of life, it puts the tension between corporate and private worship in a different light. We can worship God anywhere when we are living a life that honors and glorifies him. However, we need to balance the "I" language of our private worship with the "we" language of corporate worship.

All of us need both corporate and private worship. In our weekly corporate worship services, we learn what giving God honor and glory means in light of what the church has taught for the last two-thousand-plus years. The gathering of the Christian community for worship gives focus to everything else in our lives. Our private devotions, our call to work and service, and our interactions with others all flow from that time of gathered worship:

"Let us not give up meeting together, as some are in the habit of doing, but let us encourage one another—and all the more as you see the Day approaching" (Hebrews 10:25). The weekly gathering of God's people guides and informs our private times of worship expressed during our rule of prayer time (see chapter 2, "The Discipline of Prayer") or by the way we live.

Because our corporate worship informs and enriches our private worship, it's wise to come to church prepared for worship so that we aren't distracted by those sitting near us.

Coming Prepared for Worship

As with many things in life, we get out of worship what we put into it. If we arrive at church on Sunday morning tired and distracted, expecting someone to make us feel good or to entertain us with good music and speaking, we will get very little out of the experience. But if we arrive rested and refreshed, ready to do our part, we are more likely to leave feeling that God's Spirit touched our spirits.

It also helps to understand everyone's role in the process. If we come to church viewing the pastor and musicians as performers and the congregation as the audience, we aren't coming to church to worship; we are coming to be entertained. In reality, God is the "audience," we who have come to worship are the actors, and the clergy and musicians prompt us in worship done for God's pleasure, not our own. What a different spin that puts on corporate worship! No longer are we allowed to plop down in a pew, visit a bit with our neighbors, check out what everyone is wearing, and wait to see how the pastor and choir "do" this week.

When we understand that our role in worship is as a "dynamic participant"—with God as the audience—we come into worship ready to focus on what we will be giving God. We will be filled with excitement to see the gathered community, prompted by the worship leaders, lift their voices in praise and adoration to the God of the universe. And we will be waiting with great anticipation to see how the audience—God—responds.

What might happen to our worshiping communities if everyone came rested and prepared to worship in that way?

Worship will teach you to speak your name
when you've forgotten who you are.
CALVIN MILLER

Enriching Our Private Times of Worship

Because our private worship times during the week flow out of and are informed by the corporate weekly gathering of God's people, we can use things from that corporate worship to enrich our private times. For example, we can expand on the bodily postures we use in corporate worship, taking them to another level that might be difficult (or pretentious) to do in the large-group format. Marti describes how she enhances her private worship time:

> One of my favorite physical positions to take on when I
> am in need of spiritual refueling is to lay myself horizon-
> tally on the floor, face down, arms outstretched. Just

holding myself downward in the form of a cross and inviting God to enter my spirit and calm my heart is often enough to bring me peace. I stay that way for several minutes, sometimes half an hour, quieting my mind. I do not seek words, though sometimes they come. I do not focus on prayer, though sometimes it happens. I also don't reserve this prone posture just for Saturday night in preparation for Sunday services. In fact, I use it frequently—including in hotel rooms, maybe especially in hotel rooms, where I spend a good part of my life. It is a physical stance that allows me to keep connected to my Lord and Savior in a secure and special way. It is interesting to me that the more I try to empty my brain, the more my mouth fills with words of praise for the goodness of God, language that seemingly comes of its own volition.

If you are struggling with understanding worship outside of a Sunday morning context, experiment with different positions during your Bible reading and meditation times: Try kneeling or standing or lying prone on the floor.

As you have your private times of worship and study during the week, work to remember one or two things that impressed themselves on you during the corporate worship service from the week before. And as you come to the corporate worship service, try to find a theme from your week's private times of worship and study that may be tied into the themes for that day. Seek to view all of life as an opportunity to give God honor and glory.

PRACTICING THE DISCIPLINE

Use some of the following suggestions to make worship a discipline of joy in your life.

1. Starting Saturday evening, begin your preparations for worship. Plan what you are going to wear in the morning. Lay out your Bible or prayer book or whatever else you need to bring to worship. If you know what Scripture passages your pastor will be speaking from, read them so that during the night, the Holy Spirit can begin the work of preparing your heart and mind as good soil for planting the seed of the Word.

2. Experiment with setting aside twenty-four hours between Saturday night and Sunday night as a true Sabbath rest. At six o'clock on Saturday night, stop doing work or chores, and begin a time of relaxation, rest, and play that will last until six o'clock on Sunday night. Impossible, you say. Maybe with the schedule you have right now, but consider gradually changing your schedule over the next several months so that you could have this kind of restorative time. See how it impacts your corporate worship time as well as the rest of your week.

3. Attend your next worship service with the idea of participating fully. Let the music draw you in closer to the Holy of Holies, to the divine mystery of Father, Son, and Holy Spirit. Let the message speak to your heart rather than function as a learned lecture that you evaluate for its style of delivery. Let the Scripture reading become God talking directly to you. Think of it in terms of your life and no one else's. Picture yourself acting in a

drama that God is watching. Even if you feel self-conscious about your singing ability, participate in worship with a strong voice. Worship actively. Realize that your self-consciousness may be a form of pride. If this is a new stance toward worship for you, assess how this impacted your view of the service.

4. Catch yourself every time you start to complain about something in the worship service. Keep a record of those times, using it as the beginnings of a prayer journal for you and the worship leaders at your church to learn what it means to give God glory and honor in all that you do.

5. We know that Jesus went to parties, and he took time alone for prayer (see John 2:1-10; Matthew 14:23). He went regularly to worship at synagogues and the temple, and he also dined and visited with friends (see Mark 1:21; Luke 10:38). In other words, he interspersed the sacred with the secular in his own example of an earthly life well lived. Commit to being the same person throughout the week that you want people to believe you are on Sunday morning. Watch the way you speak and act in sporting events, shopping malls, at home with your children and spouse, and driving on the highways. Pay attention to the words and actions you engage in when you think no one is looking.

TEACHING THE DISCIPLINE

Worship with your children at home. After dinner on Saturday night, read the Scripture for worship tomorrow (if you know what it is) and sing a song that might fit those readings or the season of the church year (a carol during Advent and Christmas, for example). Or sing a song before bedtime prayers. Singing can help quiet your children's minds and transition them into praying. In addition:

EARLY CHILDHOOD (*ages 4–7*):

1. Take your children with you to corporate worship, even if the service runs concurrently with Sunday school. Sit near the front where they can see all that is happening. Require them to sit quietly. If you must take a restless, noisy child out, deal with the situation and bring him or her back in right away. It will take a few weeks, but your children will learn that church is a place to stay and participate in appropriately.

2. Teach your children to stand when the other worshipers stand and to sing when everyone else sings. Don't let them color during the prayers. Insist they stop and participate with the posture appropriate to your tradition. The earlier children develop worship habits, the stronger those habits will become ingrained. It will also keep kids more interested in and connected to what's happening around them.

   Have some quiet toys or games reserved just for church use. Pull them out only during the sermon.

3. Give young children their own age-appropriate Bible for use during the service. Help them find Scripture references as the worship leader cites them.

4. Place your kids in the children's choir if your church has one. This will teach them early on to help lead worship. In liturgical churches, this will also help them learn the liturgy, seasons of the church year, and other facts about that style of worship.

Don't clap after they sing, as that might confuse them into thinking that leading worship is a form of entertainment.

5. Take as much rush and confusion out of Sunday morning as you can. Have your kids take baths on Saturday and help them lay out their clothes for the next morning. Try to prevent Sunday mornings from turning into a frenzy of last-minute preparation that can lead to pitched family battles as you try to leave on time. If possible, use from Saturday night until Sunday night as a time of family rest and play.

MIDDLE CHILDHOOD (*ages 8–11*):

1. Talk with your children about the difference between entertainment and worship. Help them understand that church isn't supposed to be for our entertainment and isn't about making us feel good, though it often does. Whenever your children "don't get anything out of worship," ask them what they thought was missing. Teach them what being an active participant in worship means. Find an example, if you can, from their own lives that illustrates the principle that we often get out of something what we put into it.

2. Research with your children the history of a symbol used in the church, such as the cross or *ichthys*, the simple drawing of a fish used by early Christians to identify each other in secret. Christian symbols are powerful tools for getting us in touch with the Lord, who inspired their creation. Many people have *ichthys* stickers on their cars. Others—presumably not of the Christian faith—have bumper stickers that

are Darwin caricatures of them. Discuss with your children why the Darwin misrepresentation of the *ichthys* is not in the least bit funny. The answer lies in the turning on its head of a powerful Christian symbol dating back to ancient times when it had a very worshipful connotation. Compare this to how people would feel if someone made an insulting cartoon out of the Jewish Star of David. Would they find such a characterization funny? Why should the *ichthys* be treated any differently?

3. Keep your Sunday mornings sacred. This means it is a time for God and togetherness, not a time for undertaking organized team sports activities or for accepting party invitations. When necessary and appropriate, take a stand against Sunday being another weekend day to schedule things in.

4. Intentionally cultivate a relationship with another family in your faith community that has children close in age to yours. When your children arrive at church or youth programs, they will see familiar faces they enjoy. Also, there will be another family modeling godly living for your children to look up to.

ADOLESCENCE *(ages 12–15):*

1. Encourage young adults to volunteer for leadership roles in the church service. Many churches allow young teens to help serve as ushers. It is important that they participate fully in the service and not use this opportunity as an excuse to hang out with their friends in the narthex until it is time to collect the offering. If your church has a choir, encourage your teens to be in it. Some churches allow them to be altar assistants, lay

ministers, or acolytes. If there is not an obvious niche, speak with your clergy about finding a role for them.

2. When teens start to complain about the church service, turn the grumbles into a discussion of theology or worship styles. In fact, study with them other forms of worship, including taking trips together to visit other churches. Consider going to witness other religions in worship.

3. Help your adolescent youngsters organize themselves with homework and other commitments such that they can go to worship relaxed and better prepared. Find a substitute to the late nights and Sunday sporting events that will honor their growing independence but still make worship a priority.

4. If your church is sacramental, teach your adolescents what it means to take Communion or be baptized. If they are in a formal instruction program, such as confirmation, engage them in conversation about the material they are studying.

5. Encourage teens to attend church-related youth camps where you know and trust the leaders and counselors in charge. If there is a weekly youth program, encourage your youngsters to participate. Help them make church friends as well as school friends. Have the youth leaders to your home, thereby establishing a critical link to other Christian adults for your children. Because they are in the natural stage of looking to others outside the home for advice and guidance, do all you can to make sure they are looking to Christian adults and youth as much as possible.

THE BOTTOM LINE

Through the Discipline of Worship, we seek to abolish the line between sacred and secular and to view every moment of every day as an opportunity to worship God. This discipline helps us infuse our times of worship with new depth and energy by changing the way we prepare for worship and by putting worship in the context of a Sabbath rest. In practicing this discipline, we create a lifetime of holy habits that we can also instill in our children.

Chapter Eleven

THE DISCIPLINE OF GUIDANCE

For this God is our God for ever and ever;
he will be our guide even to the end.

PSALM 48:14

UNDERSTANDING THE DISCIPLINE

The Discipline of Guidance calls us to rely on friendships with other believers to help us better discern God's will. Through it, we hold a more confident sense of spiritual direction.

For years, my husband and I (Marti) belonged to a small group with three other couples. We met weekly and studied the Bible; talked intimately about our spiritual, personal, and work lives; went on outings together to dinner and sometimes the theater; played board games in each other's homes and laughed boisterously; and in general, grew to become inseparable friends. An important feature of the group's purpose was consulting one another for guidance about difficult matters that either an individual or couple was facing.

One issue in my life at the time was a troubling work situation. I felt crippled, discounted, and ripped apart on a daily basis. I began suffering from long periods of insomnia and painful bouts of stomach cramping that doubled me over. But because I was certain

God had led me to the job I held then, I felt conflicted as to whether or not he wanted me to remain in it to bring about whatever change I could, despite the physical manifestations of my emotional misery.

Our small group prayed continually for me, patiently talking through the issues time after time, trying to understand the details of my position and help me clear away clouds of doubt about how best to move forward. Finally, the group consensus was that I needed to seek other employment, and when I readily found another job that respected the talents and skills I brought, all of us knew that the clear light of truth had pointed me in the right direction. God did not require me to indefinitely endure difficult circumstances.

If the highest aim of a captain were to preserve his ship,
he would keep it in port forever.

St. Thomas Aquinas

Others Enable Discernment

As I learned through our precious small group of friends, all of us need to have people with whom we can process decisions. In order to master this discipline, we must give up prideful independence. We often hide our true feelings and thoughts from others, which sometimes results in being less than honest with God. And without an intimacy with God that faces all things frankly and openly, our spiritual lives will go flat. By practicing intimacy with others and soliciting their prayerful guidance on important life issues, we are enabled to meet our Creator on the same increasingly familiar plane.

The Discipline of Guidance requires practice with others in much the same way a company or business functions as it grows to maturity. It is impossible for a successful business to rest on the shoulders of a single human being, no matter how charismatic and competent the person. It requires and indeed depends upon the collaborative efforts of everyone in the organization. In much the same way, guidance requires the collaboration of fellow believers.

Guidance can come through any caring faith-based community, including that of psychiatrists and psychologists who believe in the same God we do. Some Christians don't like to admit there are occasions in life when medical intervention is needed for emotional or mental problems, but denial can lead to tragedy, such as in the following example.

A college student in a leadership position on his Christian college campus trusts in image only, particularly the twin images of being in control and of being a confident Christian leader, which gains him praise from those in authority. His self-loathing takes over when he knows the image to be not only false but also entirely different from the person behind it. How awful to lose the admiration of others, he thinks. On what ground would his life then stand? He kills himself because he cannot bring himself to confide to anyone what he's really feeling.

As illustrated in the story (a true one), shame and embarrassment over being finite and weak can kill and often does, especially among young people, whose suicide rate is growing in alarming proportions. If we neglect the guidance available to us in well-selected psychiatric specialists and counselors—and if we somehow imply to our children that weaknesses and worries must be kept silent and hidden away from public view—we truncate God's ability to work with very troubled souls.

Be prepared for Truth at all hours and in the most
fantastic disguises. This is the only safety.

Christopher Morley

Corporate Guidance Has Its Limits

Of course, we must be wise about the community we are looking to for guidance. We have all heard the sad stories of those who believed too securely in certain leaders and thereby gave up or at least subsumed their own God-given free will. David Koresh was a charismatic leader whose compelling but misguided rhetoric, which he believed to be Christian, helped create a staunch band of followers called "Students of the Seven Seals," sometimes known as the Branch Davidians. These people were willing to commit their children to Koresh's enigmatic cause without knowing more about him than that his personality exuded authority.[1] Jim Jones, quite sure that he was following God's commandments, held so much influence over his followers that they willingly drank poisoned Kool-Aid, mothers even ladling it into the mouths of their babies, knowing the price of death they were about to pay for following their leader's command.[2] Fanatic cultism spells danger—period. The Discipline of Guidance has nothing in common with such wickedness.

The converse side—and equally wrongheaded—is the person who decides to govern his or her life with no advice from anyone else. Ferociously independent individuals go it alone. Both of us are aware (and we expect you are too) of people who have isolated themselves from others, often for decades. They tend to live alone, engage in no customary work outside of the home, take on no regularly scheduled activities, and seek little meaningful contact with family or neighbors. When people with these characteristics fall ill or face other problems, they have few resources upon which to draw.

How do we find spiritual balance between these two extremes of behavior? The Discipline of Guidance is intended to serve for good, not evil, purposes. It intends to keep our free will intact. Even after a group of trusted advisers offers counsel, we can either take or reject their advice, depending on whether their input matches what we believe God has been saying to us. As Dallas Willard points out:

> The conscious seeking of divine guidance is safe and
> sensible only within that life of experiential union with
> God in his Kingdom that Jesus Christ brought to light. . . .
> Only our communion with God provides the appropriate
> context of communication between us and him.[3]

The corporate guidance we receive needs to complement the communication between God and us as individuals. In order to keep the channels of communication with God open, we would be wise to strengthen our unity with God through regular times of worship and prayer.

Make a habit of two things — to help or,
at least, to do no harm.

HIPPOCRATES

Resting in the Reliability of the Holy Spirit

Discerning what God may be leading us to do is that peculiar act of learning to see the unseen and of transporting ourselves into God's realm and becoming aware, in a minimally human way, of what he knows. Such discernment then becomes an act of faithful confidence in the outcome of whatever decision we make, even a decision fraught with peril, because the Holy Spirit will continue to guide us with our choices and the circumstances that inevitably spring from those choices. In other words, even if things don't go smoothly and it looks as if we made a wrong choice in the direction we are now headed, God will be there to cover our backs. The gift of the Holy Spirit is a very real and always present guide as we encounter different decisions and make new choices.

To some, this idea that all may not be smooth sailing, even when we are following God's will exactly, is frightening. To others, especially those who regularly practice the Discipline of Guidance, it's enormously reassuring. The Holy Spirit is with us in the here and now, abiding with us even as we write this book and as you read it. When we contemplate what we will do this evening or tomorrow, when we speak to our children about dinner or school, and when we kiss our spouse or encourage our neighbor, the Holy Spirit is there beside us, prepared to guide and appropriately direct our thoughts and actions.

We must ask our Father in heaven, through continual prayer, to help us become more attuned to the Holy Spirit's ways of working in our lives and to provide us with daily guidance through the Holy Spirit, which Jesus has promised will travel with us always, the Counselor who will be with us forever (see John 14:15-17; Mark 1:8).

PRACTICING THE DISCIPLINE

We all want certain and specific guidance from the Lord of the universe. If only we could be sure we are doing God's will! This is a discipline we covet because of our tremendous needs, and it requires practice—lots of it—to build our confidence in the reality of the leading readily available to us through the Holy Spirit.

1. Ask yourself, *Do I really believe God can speak to me?* Think of an example in which you heard God clearly guiding you in some direction. If you can't think of one, commit to ten minutes a day of complete solitude for the purpose of listening for God's voice. God, requiring of you few words at this point, understands your prayer. Take on a purely listening attitude, nothing more.

   You are listening for one of two things (perhaps you will be rewarded with both). One is a specific memory of a precise time and place in which God clearly guided you in a certain direction, which you faithfully followed. Reflect on how this direction affected the course of your life. The second is guidance God wants to give you now. Maybe you are wrestling with an issue, or maybe you are too complacent in your own comfortable life. Maybe you, like many of us, have slipped into self-satisfaction. Perhaps the "Hound of Heaven," as poet Francis Thompson calls God,[4] is exhorting you to do something more or different with whatever time is available to you. Be open if your listening exercise results in a distinct prod from God's holy thumb.

2. Keep a record of all the times you feel guided by Scripture readings, other people, "coincidences" (which my mother always calls "God-incidences"), music, literature, artwork, and additional interactions. After a week, review the record. Do you see a pattern? If you felt you heard nothing, ask yourself how much time in quiet contemplation you were able to spend during the week. Is it possible that God is speaking but that you are too busy to stop and listen? Or are you expecting him, through the Holy Spirit, to speak in only one way and so are missing other avenues by which his voice might reach you?

3. Examine yourself in relation to your community. Who are your good friends? Why are they good friends? Are there others in your life offering you significant help? Who are they? Write down every name that comes to mind. As you focus on the Discipline of Guidance, give yourself permission to invite others to offer you guidance, especially if you are not in the habit

of seeking help when you're faced with difficult decisions. Ask yourself how an attitude of isolation manifests itself in your life. How much do you trust your current faith community? Why, or why not? What is missing, if you feel something is? How can you personally help add that missing ingredient? How satisfied are your children with their church and Sunday school experiences? Is their satisfaction reason enough to stay, or is their dissatisfaction reason enough to leave your present church home?

4. When you are seeking guidance on an upcoming decision or situation, try assuming a position of supplication to hear God better and learn more about the guiding presence of the Holy Spirit in your own life. Get on your knees or raise your hands high to heaven or become prone on the floor, arms outstretched from your shoulders so that you form the shape of a cross.

TEACHING THE DISCIPLINE

As parents, we can earn the trust of our children by being consistent, honest, loving, and respectful, so that during critical decision times, they will come to us for guidance because they see us as their first and most dependable community. Of course, kids will also process their struggles with friends and other trusted adults, especially as they grow older, but we can lay the groundwork for shared guidance from the minute our children enter our lives.

This requires us to be somewhat vulnerable with our kids, especially when it comes to choices we're facing. They must see us pray, talk with our spouse, consult our friends, and counsel with clergy. We must teach them, bit by bit, how to approach and make decisions, just as we teach them step-by-step how to ride a bike, swim the breaststroke, and drive a car.

EARLY CHILDHOOD *(ages 4–7):*

1. Give kids in the early childhood age range a small allowance. Insist that they save 10 percent for Jesus and another 10 percent in their piggy bank for their own future use. Allow them to make here-and-now choices with the rest of the money. After the "Jesus money" has built up a bit, hold a family discussion about a community need it could meet or a charity it could be donated to, and then send it on its way. Be sure to add some of your own money to the cause so it becomes a true family gift.

   Likewise, when children's piggy bank savings build up, discuss with them what they might like to spend it on: toys, candy, a fun pair of sunglasses? Brainstorm together some of their choices, and make a list of all items down one side of a piece of paper with a plus sign and minus sign at the top. With your children securely tucked at your side, discuss and write down the plusses and minuses of each possible purchase. How will it help your children? How might it take away from something else they are already doing or render obsolete or redundant something already owned?

2. Take young children to a park and help them learn the basics of a sport, such as baseball or soccer. Coach them in ways to hold their feet, hands, elbows, and knees so that they are more apt to connect with the ball and send it where they want to

send it rather than simply connect with it via an indiscriminate bonk or plunk. You can also just play catch to help them know how to use a baseball glove and coordinate the movement of their eyes with the arc of the ball coming toward them. Teach them how to throw overhand and underhand.

In doing this, you are providing guidance, and your kids are benefiting from that guidance. It will appear that you are helping them learn a sport or two they will enjoy throughout their young lives, and that's true. But the goal here is really twofold: (a) have fun with your kids—always, and (b) help them learn to rely on you for instruction and help. You are the parent, the experienced adult, the leader they need, and it is important to foster in your children the habit of coming to you for advice and direction. A sport is often the way for this to start becoming ingrained.

3. Read a story together about a parent and child. If you don't know one, ask your public librarian for help. There are oodles of these stories out there. After you've concluded the story, discuss how the parent (or grandparent) helped the child learn more about the world. Talk about why it is important to depend on parents and older family members. Then reread the story together with this new perspective in mind.

MIDDLE CHILDHOOD (ages 8–11):

1. Identify a small decision that needs to be made, such as which video the family will watch, what game to play, or what to eat. Start with a short prayer for unity, and then begin discussing

with your children what the options are. (Set some boundaries before this activity begins. Boundaries could include the movie's rating, cost of the food, or time of night when starting a long game.) Don't act until everyone has agreed on the final choice. Watch carefully so that no one feels coerced or as if he or she must give in for "the sake of peace and quiet." Work to make this a true consensus decision, even if the final outcome takes a while to arrive at. As the family leader, you are guiding the group conversation so it is fair to all concerned. Never relinquish your role in such discussions.

2. Maps and globes usually fascinate kids in middle childhood. Have your child plot out the next trip you plan to take as a family, or make it a fictitious trip. If, for example, you were going to see all the places Laura Ingalls Wilder lived during her lifetime, what states and towns would you go to? Ask your child to locate and connect them on a map to provide a visual representation of where you would travel. Or, if you own a Bible with maps, go to those pages and plot out Jesus' life or locate biblical cities and towns that are in today's news. Then discuss the value of guidance by asking questions such as: What sorts of guidance do maps, globes, and atlases provide us? What can we learn by consulting references outside of ourselves? How does this broaden our ability to see beyond our own small piece of the world's geography? When we need other sorts of help beyond what we can find from maps, where or to whom can we go? Why is it important that we rely on authoritative human resources to help us learn more?

Adolescence (*ages 12–15*):

1. Those in this age group are ready to become guides for younger brothers and sisters or cousins. Find young children your adolescents can tutor or teach something significant to. This could include practice in writing names or learning the sounds of the alphabet. It also could be a sport or other physical activity that requires training to reach mastery, such as bouncing a ball in one position over and over again or walking while bouncing a ball. It might be riding a bike, tying shoes, sitting quietly with binoculars and watching birds or squirrels to learn more about their habits, collecting certain kinds of shells along the seashore, or gathering specific kinds of rocks on a hike.

   The point is to have your older children act as the nature guide or sports coach or academic tutor to someone considerably younger. Help teens find resources and supplies for working with a child at a developmental level considerably lower than their own. And most important, be sure to process the experience with them.

   What kinds of why and how questions did the younger child ask them? How did it feel to have to supply the answers to every question? Did your children enjoy the experience? Why, or why not? Were some of the questions too difficult to answer? Were there times your teens wished they had someone along with even more experience who could help provide answers?

   Through this discussion, you are facilitating their internalization of the difficult but rewarding role of becoming a decision maker. It is important for your kids to understand the satisfaction, hard work, and tremendous responsibility that comes with offering the most appropriate guidance possible to an individual who needs it.

2. On a regular basis, adolescents go through relationship dilemmas that cause great angst. Let none of us ever forget how tough puberty is! Kids at this age need our steadying guidance more than ever. On the other hand, they are more resistant to us because of their growing independence. All of this provides an excellent, though difficult, opportunity for real closeness and direction to occur between parents and children. Fine lines have to be trod, but larger moral discussions are often the antidote for what ails confused teens.

   If you have worked on healthy family bonding throughout their childhood, it can and must resurface for your young teens in a new and necessary way. There are so many questions during these years that begin with, "What do I do about . . . ?" or "How should I act when . . . ?" No matter their guise, such questions boil down to this one: "What's the right thing to do?"

   Work on extending a nonjudgmental, unconditionally loving attitude, because that's the only way you will be allowed entry through your teens' psychic doors. But move through them you must so that your precious children do not lose their way, buffeted on every side by the emotional tsunamis of adolescence with who-knows-what type of guidance if not yours. It's okay if only one parent (or grandparent, or special aunt or uncle) can navigate these treacherous waters with a teen. All it takes is one trusted adult guide in whom an adolescent can confide. You want to instill in them the habit of going to you when help is most needed. It's even possible that adolescent squalls will provide the best opportunity of your children's life for implanting the Discipline of Guidance.

THE BOTTOM LINE

The Discipline of Guidance is about improving our ability to discern God's will for our lives through the assistance of others. With the discipline comes a more confident sense of spiritual direction, which is absolutely necessary for healthful living. Cultivating a group of trusted friends with whom you can share intimate details of self and from whom you are fed improves the quality of our earthly lives as well as our spiritual ones.

Chapter Twelve

THE DISCIPLINE OF CELEBRATION

Rejoice in the Lord always. I will say it again: Rejoice!

PHILIPPIANS 4:4

UNDERSTANDING THE DISCIPLINE

Living year-round in a summer resort community brings many gifts. One of those is the work my (Valerie's) daughters had for years babysitting for various families who came year after year. One day, my youngest came home early in the evening from babysitting. She announced with awe and wonder that she was going to dress for dinner when she grew up. The family she was working for had just done that, and she was so impressed that the grandparents and the adult children with their spouses would view a simple barbeque in the backyard as a special time that required nicer clothes than those worn during the day.

This family was a witness to the way the Discipline of Celebration works in our lives. Every moment has the potential to be lifted up and sanctified by our attitudes and actions. Indeed, every moment holds the potential for being aware of God's love. And when that happens, we are better able to show love and joy to others.

Obedience Equals Joy

You may have thought a discussion on ways to make every day special would follow the story about my daughter. If so, you may be wondering why we are bringing up the topic of obedience. How does that fit?

When I first came across the concept that obedience equals joy, I thought, *No way! That makes no sense.* But because it bothered me, the words stuck in my mind. And then one day on my regular exercise walk, the puzzle pieces came together. That morning, I observed two different dogs and their owners. In the first case, the dog was well trained. It was off-leash but clearly under voice command. Therefore, the owner could trust it to run a bit, which it was delighting in doing. This dog's tail was wagging enthusiastically and it was obviously relishing the many smells of the mountain meadow.

The second dog was not well trained. In fact, as its owner yelled futilely for it to come, it dashed pell-mell across a very busy street without even slowing down. The owner ran breathlessly after it, and I eventually lost sight of them. That dog could have been badly hurt—or worse. And while it may have looked as if it were enjoying itself, we all know how it would have felt had it been struck by some unsuspecting driver.

Obedience equals joy because when we are walking in obedience to God's commands, we are protected from so much. This is not to say that nothing bad will ever happen to us; bad things will happen because there is sin in the world. However, a lot fewer will happen when we are obedient to God's commands because we won't be bringing trouble on our own heads. There is a saying,

"Don't create your own trouble." It means don't do something you know you shouldn't. It means remember that obedience brings joy. And joy is the hallmark of the Discipline of Celebration.

In 1 John 5:3, the apostle John writes: "This is love for God: to obey his commands. And his commands are not burdensome." And Jesus himself says in John 15:10-11, "If you obey my commands, you will remain in my love. . . . I have told you this so that my joy may be in you and that your joy may be complete."

When we are walking in the light of God's commandments, we walk with freedom. We don't have to fret and worry over every thought or decision. We can enjoy each moment as it comes, trusting that God will move and guide us as necessary. Like the trained dog off-leash, we can move in joy, knowing that our Good Master is watching out for danger.

Joy is the secret possession of the Christian.
Joy overcomes our pettiness.

C. S. Lewis

Parties Don't Just Happen

Because of how good God is, we can always find something to celebrate—even in the darkest of times. Many victims of horrible circumstances have proved this truth: Corrie ten Boom, Holocaust survivor, tells of beautiful, clear, moonlit nights that she could see through the slats of her drafty prison; a friend of Nelson Mandela's, caught up in South African apartheid, recalls the scented memory of his sparse home when his mother baked bread; an AIDS patient speaks gratitude for a kind touch from a stranger who did not veer away from him in revulsion. A young cancer patient celebrates being diagnosed with cancer as a teenager, knowing she would otherwise not have become the adult she is today. Each of these people was open to seeing God's goodness in the midst of his or her suffering.

When we train ourselves, in the midst of unpleasant or difficult circumstances, to focus intentionally on the gifts God gives us, it helps us put our own lives into proper perspective. For example, I don't enjoy having my teeth worked on, but I have trained myself to thank God that I have access to dental care and to pray for those who don't. Marti says that when she feels exhausted and sees herself leaning toward self-pity, she thinks of people who are bedfast or suffering from debilitating illness and offers gratitude to God for her robust stamina.

But in our eagerness to develop gratitude, we must not "stuff" or deny negative thoughts and emotions. God asks us to be honest about how we feel, even if we are angry, frustrated, depressed, or afraid. Negative emotions like these don't mean we can't simultaneously acknowledge what we know to be true about God's goodness. We only have to look at the psalms to see examples of this. Two-thirds of them are laments, the antonym of celebrations. The label "lamentation" seems nothing more than a euphemism for raw anger, depression, frustration, grief, and despair. However, many of those lamentations imply that the author will still praise God despite how awful everything seems to be (see Psalms 13; 22; 31; 42; 43; 59; 74; 109; 140).

So as you seek to practice this discipline, be honest with yourself and God about how you feel, but don't lose sight of the bigger picture. Celebration offers us the opportunity to transform those hard places, rising above "our light and momentary troubles [that] are achieving for us an eternal glory that far outweighs them all" (2 Corinthians 4:17).

Celebration is not [only] a part of special occasions, but an ongoing awareness that every moment is special and asks to be lifted up and recognized as a blessing from on high.

HENRI NOUWEN

A Way of Thinking

We can encircle everything we do with the Discipline of Celebration. An attitude of celebration encourages us to have a spirit of gratitude for gifts, large and small, that daily come our way.

We not only celebrate holidays and special events but also the first tulips in the spring and the fiery red maple tree in the fall. We are thankful for work (especially if it is meaningful), hot running water, a choice of shoes in our closet, a pillow for our heads, the smile of a baby, and the courteous driver who allows us to merge in heavy traffic. This discipline recognizes that every gift from God gives us a reason to give thanks and celebrate the reliability of Christ in our lives.

We practice this discipline not because we feel happy but because of the supernatural reality that surrounds us. In other words, we can offer thanks for the reality of the Resurrection even while burying our loved ones or our dreams. True joy comes only from within; it's that unshakable sense that all is well with the world because God is present and at work. As Christians, we know "the end of the story." In light of this, we can choose how we will respond in every circumstance that comes our way.

Celebration is the rock at the bottom of our souls that is not affected by the storms assailing us on the surface. To be sure, seeking out that rock in the midst of a tempestuous gale takes discipline; a steady and trained hand must firmly grip the rudder when the storms rage around us. But if we can radiate true joy from a deep place in our souls, despite the external realities, we will have much to say to a stressed-out, cynical culture that knows very little of true joy. We will offer a hope that reality has more to it than what we can see or experience. We will show that it is possible to end well, facing death in confidence despite increasing limitations. We will point to signs of the Resurrection, regardless of the overwhelming sense that it is Good Friday in the world. Joy is the melody of Christ's victory, and we are invited to sing along in everything we do.

I believe people are as they think.

FRANCIS SCHAEFFER

PRACTICING THE DISCIPLINE

As Richard Foster says, celebration "is the heart of the way of Christ. He entered the world on a high note of jubilation."[1]

1. As you begin to practice this discipline, think about what nurtures you, and then do it! Is it finding time to curl up with a good book? Taking a walk in nature? Doing a craft of some kind, such as needlepoint or knitting? Playing the piano or listening to music? Playing a sweaty game of racquetball with a friend? Mark time into your calendar for the activity. Treat the time as you would a doctor's appointment: Don't miss it unless there is an emergency.

2. Read real-life stories about remarkable people, such as Dietrich Bonhoeffer and Corrie ten Boom. They modeled a faith in God's goodness (even when it was quite hidden) that endured through some of the most horrific circumstances anyone ever experienced. With these questions, reflect on their ability to find joy in small moments and to rest on truth and hopefulness:

   • How do any of us stay hopeful in the face of awful situations?

   • How can we still find the energy to smile at or reach out to another when our internal sorrow threatens to overwhelm us?

   • What is it that makes some human beings' spirits resilient? Are they more special than us? (A resounding *no* to that one! Each of us has the capacity to sustain and endure if we can focus on celebration.)

   • Is resilience perhaps defined best as the ability to celebrate small moments and tiny things, no matter what the external circumstances? Is that ability the very thing that keeps us alive and sane? (We both believe it is.)

3. Find a way to celebrate everything. Have a special dessert when you see the first robin, hummingbird, or daffodil in spring. Light

candles when you eat, even if you're just having a simple sand-
wich. Use the good dishes and silverware—just because. Organize
a croquet tournament and potluck with your neighbors. Anything
you can do to bring joy and laughter to people is worth doing.

4. Think back on a time when you were disobedient to God's call
and commands. What happened? Contrast it with a time when
you were obedient. How did that situation turn out? Explore
the feelings that you still have related to both of those events.
Are you more at ease when you are doing things right, such as
driving the speed limit, or do you like the challenge of "push-
ing the envelope," that is, seeing how much you can get away
with before getting caught, say, in a speed trap?

When you feel new peace and joy seep into your core, begin to
think how you can help others find it too. The best place to start,
of course, is with your children.

TEACHING THE DISCIPLINE

Joy is the secret treasure of all those who believe in God and
understand the spiritual disciplines. Celebration is a pearl of
immense price that we can leave as an inheritance for our children. Most of us have no problem celebrating the big, onetime
happy events in our lives; it's learning how to practice this every
day that takes discipline. We can cultivate a spirit of gratitude in
our kids by helping them discover ways to make each day special.
For example:

- Tell your children often that you love them. Don't assume they know it.
- Place little notes in your kids' lunches telling them you are thinking about them and praying for their day.
- On a nice day, load supper into the car and go on a picnic.
- Sing, even if you're not very good at it. Enjoy music, even loudly once in a while. Dance to it, even if you never learned how. Get out the crayons and color as a family some afternoon.
- Collect favorite board games and make a practice of regularly playing them as an entire family. Perhaps Santa can bring a new one each year, as he does at the Garlett house.
- Do something unexpected and fun on a dreary day. For example, an elementary teacher we know announced a beach day theme one brutally cold February. The next day, after peeling off the layers of warm clothes they had come to school in, her students decorated the classroom with sand and beach toys and wore shorts and flip-flops inside the school building. It lifted everyone's spirits. The same kinds of ideas can be done at home.
- While the Discipline of Celebration does not have to involve spending money, there are times when we buy memories. Marti once inherited ten thousand dollars that she used to fund a family vacation. I take my girls every year to a water theme park that is expensive, but it is a day everyone looks forward to.

Psalm 84:5 says, "Happy are those whose strength is in you, in whose heart are the highways to Zion" (NRSV). The "highways to Zion" are things that draw us closer to the transcendent goodness of God—activities, and relationships that refresh and restore us and bring deep peace to our lives. We must help develop the highways to Zion in our children's lives so that they may travel from childhood into adulthood with as much joy and gladness as possible. Besides the previously mentioned general "highway building" ideas, you can try the following age-specific ones.

EARLY CHILDHOOD *(ages 4–7):*

1. Start a gratitude journal. Each night at bedtime, gather your kids and write down big and small things that you all are thankful for. When they are struggling with a bad day or situation, pull out the gratitude journal and use it to prime the pump in looking for God's hand in the midst of the frustrations.

2. Help your children to be honest about their feelings, especially negative ones. Encourage them not to "stuff" or deny their feelings or to deal with anger in passive-aggressive ways. Find ways for them to appropriately express anger. Some examples are throwing rocks in a rock pile or getting their anger out by throwing aluminum cans in the containers at the recycling center. If your children get frustrated with someone, have them draw a picture of that person or write a letter that expresses how they feel. Then, crumple up the paper and toss it in the trash. Any safe but very physical activity that vents frustration is wonderfully cathartic. Teach your kids to unload negative

thoughts and feelings along the way instead of letting them
build up to the breaking point.

3. Help them write thank-you notes for gifts they have received.
   Have them draw a picture and dictate to you what they want to
   say if they can't yet write the letter themselves, but have them
   sign their own names.

MIDDLE CHILDHOOD (ages 8–11):

1. This age group can write their own thank-you notes. Not only
   is this exercise common courtesy and good manners, it also
   teaches kids that gratitude takes time. Get them some fun
   paper and simple art supplies to decorate the note.

2. Read Revelation 21 and 22 to your children. Help them to
   understand "the end of the story." The final book in C. S.
   Lewis's CHRONICLES OF NARNIA series, *The Last Battle*, is excellent for presenting this idea to children of all ages.

3. Once a month during the school year, take each of your kids to
   lunch individually. This can be as simple as a picnic in the
   park. One of the greatest gifts we can give our children is
   showing them regularly that we enjoy spending time with
   them as people.

4. Find a hobby you can do together: star gazing, bird watching,
   pottery classes, learning to play the piano, taking up a sport
   such as tennis or fishing, and so on.

5. Think of a fun activity that you could do with your children,
   and invite others to join you. It could be a birthday party for
   the cat or going on a bug-and-creature walk in the woods.

6. Each week, establish your own form of family TGIF (Thank God It's Friday). Go bowling, fly a kite, make old-fashioned ice cream sodas—you are limited only by your own imagination. By all means, ensure your kids are invited to participate in deciding TGIF events.

7. Make sure your kids have a safe place to vent frustrations. In addition to the suggestions mentioned previously, other ideas for appropriately letting off steam include: using old baseball bats on tree stumps, hitting tennis balls against a wall, or running around a track for several minutes.

ADOLESCENCE *(ages 12–15)*:

Teenagers need celebration more than ever. Kids go through many emotional ups and downs and experience tremendous insecurity, even fear, during the tumultuous years between childhood and emerging adulthood. Anything you can do to help them find joy in the midst of puberty and to learn to channel anger and frustration appropriately will go a long way in helping them navigate these rough waters.

1. Look for a variety of ways to bring joy to your teens each day. Ideas include simple affirmations, notes, and spontaneous fun times together. Send an e-mail card to them at school if they have access to the Internet during the day.

2. Go with them to a movie, a miniature golf course, or an amusement park. "Kidnap them" after school and buy them an ice cream cone.

3. Help them begin to express gratitude for all the gifts of life they experience daily. Adopt a less fortunate family and then assist your adolescents in becoming actively involved with food, toy, or clothing distribution. Help your kids plan fun outings for younger children in the adopted family, such as a picnic and games in the park or a trip to see a baseball game.

4. Respond to your teens' moods with as much love and kindness as you can muster. Allow them to suffer the consequences of bad behavior, but do so with plenty of love. Show them as much as you possibly can that good overcomes bad by loving them through their difficult days. Hug them. Smile at them when you talk to them. If they think you are being unreasonable, ask them why. Listen carefully. Are you being too controlling? Is there a possible compromise to the issue?

5. Let your teens have fun with clothing and hairstyles. Being allowed some experimental freedom in those areas may keep them from feeling a need to experiment in more dangerous activities. Take a couple of hours to go to the mall. Listen to what your kids say about what they like and don't like. Have something tasty to eat or drink while you discuss a standard of modesty in clothing that is acceptable to both of you.

6. Encourage your adolescents to have a broad focus in life. Hospitals, volunteer fire departments, and park programs all need volunteers. Teens involved in activities they are interested in have better self-esteem and find life more enjoyable.

THE BOTTOM LINE

In the Discipline of Celebration, we develop a habit of gratitude for what is good in all of our circumstances and an ability to celebrate in small and simple ways. Then we can say with the apostle Paul, "For I have learned to be content whatever the circumstances. I know what it is to be in need, and I know what it is to have plenty. I have learned the secret of being content in any and every situation, whether well fed or hungry, whether living in plenty or in want" (Philippians 4:11-12).

THE END IS ONLY THE BEGINNING

May our Lord Jesus Christ himself and God our Father, who loved
us and by his grace gave us eternal encouragement and
good hope, encourage your hearts and strengthen you
in every good deed and word.

2 THESSALONIANS 2:16-17

The book is ending, but fresh adventures with your kids are just beginning. We hope that within these pages you have found new light for the journey and new pleasure in undertaking it.

We have deliberately focused on one discipline at a time to help you learn each discipline enough to implant it in your children's lives, but we do not want our chapter-by-chapter approach to keep you from seeing the connection of each discipline to all the others. If we were to chart the relationship of the disciplines to each other, it would look something like the diagram on page 196.

As this diagram shows, celebration surrounds a disciplined life. When we enact the spiritual disciplines in our own lives and help foster them in our children's lives, gladness reigns. When we live the spiritual disciplines, worship lies at the center of our existence. Who we are and what we do gives glory to God, even if what we are doing at any given moment isn't particularly religious. All the other disciplines flow between celebration and worship.

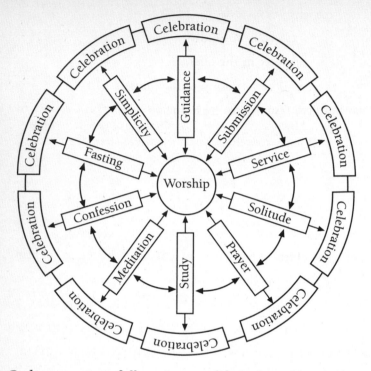

God wants us to fully enjoy our life in him. He wants us to laugh, make merry, and go through life cheerfully because of his manifold provisions for overcoming anything we face. The disciplined life is to be celebrated, fêted, treated like an ongoing party that readies us to meet Christ.

We are not saying that living a disciplined life is easy; it's not, as all who have tried it or are doing it well know. But it is, undisputedly, a way of living that is power-packed with gratification. Delight is out there in life for our plucking, if only we discipline ourselves to grasp it.

Our final prayer for you as you go forth best takes shape in the form of a traditional Scottish blessing:

If there is righteousness in the heart,

there will be beauty in the character.

If there is beauty in the character,

there will be harmony in the home.

If there is harmony in the home,

there will be order in the nation.

If there is order in the nation,

there will be peace in the world.

So let it be.[1]

CREATING A MASTER CALENDAR

1. Take a large sheet of paper and turn it so the longer side is on top and the shorter sides are in your right and left hands. Write the days of the week across the top. On the left side, put the time you *usually* get up in the morning at the top and the time you *usually* go to bed at the very bottom. Fill in every half hour in between. (See an example of a completed Master Calendar on the next page.)

2. Block out time for fixed activities in your schedule. Remember to factor in round-trip travel. For example, if you work an eight-to-five day but have a half-hour commute each way, then you need to block out 7:30 A.M. to 5:30 P.M. for each workday. Extra time also needs to be added to educational commitments, Bible study groups, piano lessons, physical therapy appointments, carpooling times, worship services, choir rehearsals, and so on. Include the time it takes to travel there, change clothes, set up, or whatever. If you have activities you do once a month or every other week, pick your busiest week during a typical month and base the Master Calendar on that week.

3. Next—and this is the most critical step—block out time for everything you do to keep body and soul together: exercise, grocery shopping, laundry, lawn and car care, housecleaning. Even if you don't do these at the same time or day every week,

Time	MONDAY	TUESDAY	WEDNESDAY	THURSDAY	FRIDAY	SATURDAY	SUNDAY
6:30							
7:00							
7:30	Morning Routine:						
8:00	Includes Bible reading, exercise walk, showering/dressing, breakfast, reading a newspaper, checking e-mails, feeding the						
8:30							
9:00	cat, and straightening up the house as needed						
9:30							Church
10:00	Housecleaning	Grocery Shop	Work at Home: National Board	Laundry	Work	Work at Home	Includes Driving Time To and From
10:30	Housecleaning	Errands	Writing Projects	Work at Home:	Includes Driving Time	or	
11:00	Laundry	Put Groceries Away		Various Commitments,		Playtime	
11:30	Laundry			Projects	To and From	(Flexible)	
NOON	Menu Planning	Work	Work	Includes Driving Time			
12:30	Menu Planning	Includes Driving Time	Includes Driving Time	To and From			
1:00	Plant Watering	To and From	To and From				
1:30							
2:00	Weekly Calendar						
2:30	Review with John						
3:00					Work at Home:		
3:30				Work and	Various Commitments,		
4:00				Two Rehearsals	Projects		
4:30	Fun		Travel Time	Includes Driving Time			
5:00	Time	Dinner Prep	Dinner with John Downtown	To and From			
5:30		or			Dinner Includes Prep and Cleanup		
6:00	with						
6:30	John	Monthly Meeting	Two Rehearsals				
7:00			Downtown				
7:30							
8:00							
8:30							
9:00							
9:30							
10:00	Bedtime Routine & Reading	Bedtime Routine & Reading	Bedtime Routine & Reading	Bedtime Routine & Reading	Bedtime Routine & Reading	Bedtime Routine & Reading	Bedtime Routine & Reading

This is a copy of my (Valerie's) current Master Calendar. It includes (1) all of my regularly scheduled work time, both at home and at church, (2) my "body and soul" time, which includes housework, dinner, exercise, and Bible reading, and (3) discretionary time for tasks such as reading, writing projects, taking the occasional nap, and spending time with my family and friends. The blank spaces allow a bit of flexibility for rearrangement of my weekly tasks for those times when a fun invitation is extended or an unexpected emergency happens.

find a reasonable day and time and block it out. Remember to factor in travel time and extras such as putting the groceries away, folding clothes, and driving to the car wash.

Take your time on this step, as these activities tend to make or break us. If you don't have clean clothes, healthy meals, and time for rest and renewal, you will likely become stressed and irritable.

4. Finally, block out time for anything else you do that hasn't been covered in the previous categories: phone calls for organizations, hobbies you do on a regular basis, piano practicing, and so on. Again, even if you don't do these at a fixed time each week, find a realistic time and day for them on the calendar.

   What does this Master Calendar tell you? Are there any blank spots? Do many of your open times correspond with the open times of your spouse and children? What does this exercise tell you about your current lifestyle?

5. Pray about your calendar. If it is filled from morning until late at night, commit to concrete steps to unload some of your commitments. Review the steps on learning to say "no" in the Discipline of Simplicity on pages 89–90. Write out a plan of action and post it in a prominent place. If you have a lot of blank spaces on your calendar, pray about what God may be calling you to do.

6. Finally, hang the Master Calendar near the phone. When someone calls and invites you to participate in something new, look at your calendar. If the time slot is occupied, even with something like laundry, you can honestly say, "I already have a

commitment then." If it's something you really want to do, ask yourself where you can make changes in the calendar to find a suitable spot for the activity or chore that is currently marked there. If you can't, maybe you shouldn't take on the new activity in this season of your life. Remember, only God is infinite and can do everything at once.

NOTES

CHAPTER 2

1. Marc Dunaway, comp., *Building a Habit of Prayer* (Ben Lomond, Calif.: Conciliar Press, 1989), p. 14.
2. *Book of Common Prayer* (New York: Oxford University Press, 1990), p. 458.

CHAPTER 3

1. Richard J. Foster, *Celebration of Discipline: The Path to Spiritual Growth* (San Francisco: Harper & Row, 1978), pp. 49–51.

CHAPTER 4

1. Richard J. Foster, *Devotional Classics: Selected Readings for Individuals and Groups*, ed. James Bryan Smith (San Francisco: Harper & Row, 1993).
2. Dallas Willard, *In Search of Guidance: Developing a Conversational Relationship with God* (San Francisco: Harper & Row, 1993), p. 172.

CHAPTER 7

1. Richard J. Foster, *Celebration of Discipline* (HarperSanFrancisco, 1988), p. 98.

CHAPTER 8

1. Richard J. Foster, *Celebration of Discipline: The Path to Spiritual Growth* (San Francisco: Harper & Row, 1978), p. 112.
2. Foster, pp. 112–113.
3. Joanna Weaver, *Having a Mary Heart in a Martha World* (Colorado Springs, Colo.: WaterBrook, 2000), p. 8.

CHAPTER 9

1. Oswald Chambers, *My Utmost for His Highest* (Dodd, Mead, 1935), p. 101.

CHAPTER 10
1. Oswald Chambers, *My Utmost for His Highest* (Dodd, Mead, 1935), p. 6.

CHAPTER 11
1. http://www.courttv.com/onair/shows/mugshots/indepth/koresh.html.
2. http://www.crimelibrary.com/notorious_murders/mass/Jonestown/index_1.html.
3. Dallas Willard, *In Search of Guidance: Developing a Conversational Relationship with God* (HarperSanFrancisco, 1993), pp. 23–24.
4. A. H. E. Lee, ed., and D. H. Nicholson, comp., *The Oxford Book of English Mystical Verse* (Oxford University Press, 1917), p. 239.

CHAPTER 12
1. Richard J. Foster, *Celebration of Discipline: The Path to Spiritual Growth* (San Francisco: Harper & Row, 1978), p. 163.

EPILOGUE
1. "If There Is Righteousness in the Heart," http://www.fife.50megs.com/celtic-blessings2.htm.

ABOUT THE AUTHORS

VALERIE E. HESS is a pastor's wife, mother, teacher, retreat speaker, and musician. Her husband of twenty-eight years, John, is an associate pastor at First Presbyterian Church in Boulder, Colorado. They have two grown daughters.

Valerie has been actively involved with Renovaré. She brought the program to First Presbyterian Church, wrote a monthly newsletter for it for several years, and organized a regional Renovaré conference in Boulder. She has taught yearlong adult Sunday school classes, workshops, and retreats on the spiritual disciplines.

Valerie also is on the national board for the Leadership Program for Musicians Serving Small Congregations (LPM), a continuing education program for "undertrained" church musicians. She received her master's in church music and organ from Valparaiso University, has a bachelor's in music and psychology from Metropolitan State College in Denver, and is currently the coordinator of music ministries and the organist for Trinity Lutheran Church in Boulder.

※ ※ ※

MARTI WATSON GARLETT, Ph.D., is dean of the Teachers College at Western Governors University, where she has developed the first accredited, competency-based online teacher preparation programs in the U.S.

Marti began her career as a pre-K–8 classroom teacher and taught in public schools in urban, suburban, and rural settings. She also served for a decade as the television teacher "Miss Marti" on the syndicated children's program *Romper Room*. In addition, she is a citizen of the world, having taught on five continents and traveled extensively through twenty-eight countries. She has written two other books, *Who Will Be My Teacher?* and *Kids with Character*, and speaks at national meetings throughout the United States. Her master's degree is from Peabody College of Vanderbilt University and her doctorate from Claremont Graduate University.

Marti and her husband make their home in Los Angeles, California. They are parents to two grown sons who both live nearby with their own burgeoning families.

MORE SPIRITUAL DISCIPLINE BOOKS FOR MOM AND DAD.

Soul Guide

Discover a deeper sense of spiritual direction and guidance from biblical characters, contemporaries, and Jesus' ministry.

by Dr. Bruce Demarest
1-57683-286-4

When the Soul Listens

Feeling as if God isn't speaking to you? Build a lasting connection with God as you discover spiritual direction through contemplative living that will lead you to rest and guidance in Him.

by Jan Johnson
1-57683-113-2

Spiritual Disciplines for the Christian Life

Drawn from Scripture and godly Christian lives, this book is a guide to disciplines that can deepen your walk with God.

by Donald S. Whitney
1-57683-027-6

To get your copies, visit your local bookstore, call 1-800-366-7788, or log on to www.navpress.com. Ask for a FREE catalog of NavPress products. Offer BPA.

NAVPRESS ®
BRINGING TRUTH TO LIFE
www.navpress.com